FIGHTING THE WAR OF IDEAS LIKE A REAL WAR

MESSAGES TO DEFEAT THE TERRORISTS

Fighting the War of Ideas like a Real War

Messages to Defeat the Terrorists

J. Michael Waller

THE INSTITUTE OF WORLD POLITICS PRESS
WASHINGTON

THE INSTITUTE OF WORLD POLITICS PRESS

Published in the United States of America
by The Institute of World Politics Press
1521 16th Street NW, Washington DC 20036 USA

www.iwp.edu

ISBN-13: 978-0-6151-4463-4

Some of the chapters in this book appeared in earlier form as White Papers or other products of The Institute of World Politics. Portions of the chapter on "Making Jihad Work for America" appeared in the Spring, 2006 *Journal of International Security Affairs*.

070411/070502

Academic Edition

Forthcoming IWP Press books edited by the same author:

Strategic Influence: Public Diplomacy, Counterpropaganda and Political Warfare

The Public Diplomacy Reader

For Victor

"Some of the best weapons do not shoot."

U.S. Army
Counterinsurgency Field Manual FM 3-24
December, 2006

Contents

Acknowledgements   xi

Introduction   13

Chapter 1   Wartime message-making:
             An immediate-term approach   19

Chapter 2   The importance of words   38

Chapter 3   Making jihad work for America   53

Chapter 4   Branding the enemy   76

Chapter 5   The secret weapon that's worse than death   93

Chapter 6   Spectrum of messages   110

Conclusion   145

About the author   148

About The Institute of World Politics   148

Acknowledgements

This book is the result of more than 20 years of experience observing, and at times participating in or against, insurgencies, counterinsurgencies, and regime changes. The author owes thanks to many who assisted in the work at every stage of research, writing and publication, especially John Lenczowski, President of The Institute of World Politics, who so enthusiastically supported this project. Andrew Garfield provided important editorial advice. Additional thanks are due to Mark Beall, Shawn Brimley, Mike Cohn, Jim Guirard, Bryan Hill, Jim Holmes, Amleset Kidane, Mallorie Lewis, Brian Newsome, Juliana Geran Pilon, Justin Stebbins, Charles Van Someren, Nicole Villescas and Adam Whiteley; and to people in the State Department, Defense Department and elsewhere in government for their quiet counsel.

I also want to thank my students at the Institute. Their enthusiastic independent research, questions and comments in my classes have made teaching at IWP a reward in itself. They challenged my thinking and hopefully sharpened my reasoning. Many have moved up to apply in real life what they learned in the classroom. And to everyone on the home front: Thank you.

Introduction

American decisionmakers irrespective of political affiliation seem far more comfortable with bombing people in other countries than with trying to persuade them to change their attitudes or behavior. They wonder why people in Middle East hate us when Arabic-language satellite TV channels saturate viewers with ceaseless, bloody images of maimed and slain Iraqi children and grandparents, cut down and blasted apart either by the day's bombings or Coalition operations. The sight of a child reclining placidly in a worn-out hospital bed breaks the heart when the camera lens pulls back and shows the bandaged stumps of a freshly amputated arm or leg. Few such images, to say nothing of the R-rated gore of a bombing aftermath, make it on heavily sanitized American TV.

Whether the unintended consequence of a U.S. attack on a terrorist target or the deliberate work of a suicide bomber, the reasons for the horror are lost in the noise of the loss or suffering. The relentless, daily bombardment of such searing imagery – often spun to blame the United States but frequently devoid of context – is enough to move all but the coldest soul into a seething range against the U.S. either as the instigator of the war or as the direct cause of the suffering.

Somehow, American messages of democracy and friendship don't fit in that landscape. Back in Washington, policymakers wonder why they continue to lose ground in the war of ideas or why so few in the Muslim world seem willing to speak out against terrorism. The answer is easy to find. Not in the Arab street but from the hell houses of urban combat, where American troops email back home: "The locals don't support the bad guys, but they don't openly support us, either. We're losing a fight we can win. What can we do?"

Those on the front lines realize better than most that we are losing a propaganda war and that we can and must win. The reality of course is that there is so much more that the country which brought down the Soviet Union can do to win the war of ideas. Most of measures we need to implement will take a long time to put in place. That said, there is so much that we can do now. That is why this book is not about the long-term. It's about the now. It offers a way to wage this pivotal battle in the immediate-term: Cost-effective, realistic solutions that the U.S. and its allies can implement quickly, without bureaucratic reorganization or unusual reprogramming of funds. The book's focus will not therefore be on structures and processes, but on the nature and content of the messages themselves and the positive effects that can be achieved in Iraq and around the world.

To start, we examine the end purpose of the nation's communication strategy. Is it simply a public relations tool intended to cultivate friends and build understanding? Or is it more properly a strategy for influence, where the end goal is to shape not just opinions, emotions and attitudes over the long term, but fundamentally to change beliefs, behaviors, policies and events – and defeat the enemy – now, when we need to?

We also consider the nature and content of American messages in the midst of an information-saturated world of instantaneous, swarming words and images through new internetted communication technologies. Those cheap and easily available capabilities give small groups and individuals the communicative powers once reserved for media conglomerates and governments. The individuals, officials and organizations who fail to adapt often wonder why, despite their seemingly boundless resources, their well-resourced and talented but slow public affairs spin-shops face defeat after defeat.

Public diplomacy, public affairs, information operations, PSYOP and strategic communication

The U.S. has a "secret weapon" of sorts that is so secret that policymakers don't seem to appreciate the sum of its parts. All of the capabilities need to win the war of ideas are there:

- *Public diplomacy* is defined for this book as a government's communication or interaction with the people of other countries, to influence foreign publics' perceptions and attitudes in support of national objectives. Because it involves building relations and earning trust, public diplomacy by its very nature is necessarily slow to produce results, though it can be used to advance more pressing objectives.

- *Public affairs* is generally the discipline of informing the domestic public, and the media in general, about government issues and policies. Its timeframe is much shorter than public diplomacy, geared toward more immediate news cycles.
- *Information operations*, or IO, is more strictly a military term that concerns the use of information, both systems and content, to advance tactical or operational military objectives. Its older cousin is *psychological operations*, popularly known as PSYOP, a tactical and operational military tool to influence the thoughts, emotions and actions of military adversaries and of civilians in the zones of combat.

All of the above, along with *international broadcasting* and *special operations*, are rolled into a larger, evolving discipline known as *strategic communication*. According to a pioneering government report on the matter,

> strategic communications describes a variety of instruments used by governments for generations to *understand* global attitudes and cultures, engage in dialogue of ideas between people and institutions, *advise* policymakers, diplomats and military leaders on the public opinion implications of policy choices, and *influence* attitudes and behavior through communications strategies.[1]

Understand, advise, influence. The Pentagon started its communication transformation shortly after the terrorist attacks of September 11, 2001, and led the way for the entire government with a major study in 2004. The State Department began to develop a new public diplomacy strategy in 2005. The Army and Marine Corps issued a revolutionary new counterinsurgency doctrine, published as Field Manual 3-24, in December, 2006.

Something else will speed their success: complementary measures that add heft to the positive messages with an accelerant to attack the terrorists, their allies, and other adversaries, and fight the "war of

---

[1] William Schneider, Jr., ed., *Defense Science Board 2004 Summer Study on Transition to and from Hostilities* (Office of the Under Secretary of Defense for Acquisition, Technology and Logistics, December 2004), p. 67. Emphasis in original.

ideas" not as an enterprise in global understanding, but like a real war – now, in support of our combat troops and hard-pressed diplomats.

This book is about that accelerant. It emphasizes immediate and achievable measures that complement traditional public diplomacy and quickly fill a missing link in the nation's strategic communication concept.

The State Department, which dominates the government's global message content, lists the three main elements of its evolving new strategy:

Offer people throughout the world a positive vision of hope and opportunity that is rooted in America's belief in freedom, justice, opportunity and respect for all;

Isolate and marginalize the violent extremists; confront their ideology of tyranny and hate. Undermine their efforts to portray the west as in conflict with Islam by empowering mainstream voices and demonstrating respect for Muslim cultures and contributions;

Foster a sense of common interests and common values between Americans and people of different countries, cultures and faiths throughout the world.[2]

Our accelerant is implied in this strategy: isolate and marginalize the enemy and its allies, confront their ideology and undermine their efforts. We seek an unashamedly offensive strategy to take and hold the initiative in the war of ideas. This information offensive is fought not as one would conduct diplomacy, but as one would wage true warfare: a political and psychological strategy not just to undermine the enemy but to help our diplomats and combat forces destroy it. This will be our focus.

* * *

We begin in Chapter 1 with an overarching immediate-term approach to defining the problem, overcoming certain self-imposed restrictions on how we fight the war of ideas, taking the ideological

---

[2] "Major Public Diplomacy Accomplishments, 2005-2006," Office of Public Diplomacy and Public Affairs, U.S. Department of State, December, 2006.

fight to the enemy, and combining traditional public diplomacy instruments with the attack accelerant.

Next, in Chapter 2, we explore an extremely effective weapon that costs nothing and can be deployed immediately. That weapon is words. The chapter surveys the use of words as weapons throughout history, cultural challenges and opportunities in employing effective words, our vulnerability to how the enemy uses words, and how we can take back the language from the enemy and put it to work for national purposes.

The provocatively titled Chapter 3, "Making jihad work for America," more deeply mines the issue of words in our conflict with Islamist extremism, giving specific and authoritative examples of how to determine key ideas to use in an ideological warfare campaign. These include defining common concepts in ways that are acceptable to much of our target audience in conflict areas, in order to deprive the enemy of its most central ideas while overwhelming it with alternative narratives that neutralize the attractiveness of extremist ideology.

Taking the premise further, Chapter 4 revives the idea of "branding." In this attack strategy, we brand not ourselves but the enemy. We also brand the wars we fight.

Chapter 5 covers "the secret weapon that's worse than death." Yet the weapon itself is neither secret nor lethal. It works through cultural traits in contested societies and psychological traits in the enemy camp that leave extremists vulnerable by virtue of their own need for rigidity of thought and total control of image. Culturally, the weapon has nearly universal applications. Terrorist leaders from Osama bin Laden on down have stated, publicly, that they fear this particular weapon worse than death. That weapon is ridicule.

In Chapter 6 we look at the spectrum of our target audiences, in this case, in the *ummah* or Islamic nation around the world, and probe the development of message-driven means of attack to marginalize and discredit the extremists by dividing them from one another and from their support bases.

America paradoxically finds itself taking the moral high ground in leading the fight against the terrorists and other global threats, but places itself in a weak, self-defeating and morally reprehensible situation by failing to marshal its formidable forces to persuade. In pursuing a strategy that emphasizes eliminating the direct terrorist threat rather than influencing the communities that continue to replenish the ranks, coffers and safe havens of our enemies, the U.S.

has taken unnecessary casualties, undermined its own cause and alienated existing and potential allies.

The U.S. must be unashamed of using strategic influence. Within the broad field of strategic influence, the U.S. must be equally unashamed about waging ideological warfare against the enemy. The message strategies herein offer greater diversity and more choices in the gray area between traditional diplomacy and lethal force. Indeed, this area is no longer gray but can be seen as a bright and well-defined spectrum of diverse instruments. This "new" spectrum of tools now offers the U.S. and is allies a second chance in the war against terrorism generally, the wars in Iraq and Afghanistan, and in conflicts of the future.

1

Wartime message-making: An immediate-term approach

Introduction

As the United States struggles to shape coherent messages to the world, it must also refine the means through which it delivers its ideas. The near-universal default is public diplomacy – the U.S. government's communication with the publics of the world – now combined with a larger evolving discipline called strategic communication. Yet policymakers and others lack a clear definition of how one relates to the other, or how either relates to present international political, diplomatic, military and security realities. And we are still fighting more to get the message out than waging a full-blown influence war against our enemies.

Our public diplomacy approaches and applications, while important in building long-term perceptions and relations, are inconsistent with the realities of the new international environment. Advances in information technology and the proliferation of electronic media outlets have leveled the battlespace between the U.S. and the world's small powers and non-governmental organizations. Even individuals can undermine Washington's carefully crafted messages rapidly and constantly, attacking in swarms and refuting, distorting and drowning out U.S. messages, and agitating increasingly shrill and influential opposition.

Against this background, the United States can and must reorient its approach to meet immediate-term wartime necessities. It need not wait for the crucial but time-consuming structural changes in the public diplomacy machine. Instead it can begin immediately by recalibrating its message strategy and modernizing the means of delivery.

We begin this process by asking the right questions. What are our core messages? What impact do we want to achieve? How effective have the messages truly been? How effective are they likely to be? What can we do to give those messages greater impact, right now when we need them, utilizing the people and resources we already have?

Certainly creative and capable use of information technologies can help make up for years of lost time since 9/11, and pull the nation out of its global political nosedive in a very short timeframe. That said, the technology is useless or worse (as our adversaries master it more cleverly than we in some cases) until we take a different approach toward how we communicate with the world and why. That is why answering the questions listed above is so vital.

To succeed quickly, good public diplomacy and strategic communication in support of the war effort – and larger 21st century national interests – need an accelerant. Hence the central theme of this monograph: to reorient how we communicate with the world in the short-term, accelerating the tempo and intensity of the nation's conduct of the war of ideas.

Points of departure

In order to develop successful wartime messages, we must know first what we seek to accomplish and how we wish to achieve it. If we want to win a long-term global war, then we must secure and maintain a strategic influence presence around the world to support not only the current conflict, but other issues, present and future. However, we must also win perceptions victories here and now, while our troops need them, and before extremist movements can grow any further.

Our audience, therefore, is most of the entire world: allies new and old who need reinforcement, traditional allies who no longer support us and are drifting away, neutrals whose bias or genuine neutrality we must keep or regain in our favor, soft opponents who can be made softer, and hard opponents who can be calmed, cleaved or isolated, their militancy rendered ineffective. We begin with certain understandings:

- Terrorism is a form of political and psychological warfare; it is protracted, high-intensity propaganda, aimed more at the hearts of the public and the minds of decisionmakers, and not at the physical victims;

- The positive and gentle nature of traditional public diplomacy is not well-suited to neutralize or attack such psychological and political warfare;
- The gradual, patient, long-term approach of public diplomacy is a necessity for strategic purposes, but does little to address the most pressing, near-term national needs;
- Explaining U.S. policies and culture, and non-offensive messages about American ideals, are vital but insufficient for current realities;
- Some U.S. policies and statements inadvertently benefit the enemy;
- We cannot credibly sell a bad policy, no matter how it is packaged;
- There are some issues, good and bad, that we simply cannot convince people to support, yet we must pursue them nevertheless;
- There are many other issues that people will support as long as the United States is not the messenger;
- Despite profound differences and antipathies, the U.S. and most of the Islamic world do share common interests and causes, which, it must be remembered, includes worshiping the one God, a core issue that we ignore at our peril;
- We cannot afford to wait for the cumulative effect of traditional public diplomacy to work because we have lost several years; our information initiative and our troops need the support now, and we risk running out of time in current war zones and other parts of the world.

Universality of ideology

People buy into an ideology, irrespective of its hue, for broadly the same reasons. Ideology provides people with a unifying identity and sense of community. It gives them a cause they can identify with. It provides a sense of purpose, meaning and shape to their lives. Ideology also provides someone else to blame for a people's misfortunes, and building up an image of an enemy to fight. Perhaps most importantly, ideology offers the hope that direct action will make for a better future, either in this life or the next.

Experience has shown that if we properly understand the tenets and nuances of a particular ideology, we can employ all of the tools of influence to expose the absurdity of an ideology's precepts. We can dispel the myths and lies on which the ideology is based. We can destroy the ideology's credibility and lure its supporters away by offering more tangible and realistic alternatives (even if those alternatives do not fit snugly with our own worldview). The bottom line is that an ideology such as Islamist extremism is built on foundation of sand which can be easily undermined by the right ideas and arguments, delivered via the appropriate channels. We have fought and won this type of warfare before and can do so again.

Islamism: a political ideology, not a religion

First, let's dispense with a self-made dilemma that has crippled U.S. message-making. We are not targeting a religion. Radical Islamism is an extremist political ideology. It is the politicized mutation of a religion. Radical Islamists are political extremists who seek to change or destroy an established political order by intimidation, terrorism and subversion: classical means of ideological warfare that the U.S. and other countries have successfully fought and defeated in the past.

Therefore the U.S. can combat radical Islamism freely without being concerned about fighting a religious battle. Radical Islamists work to influence international politics, foreign governments, and the internal workings of the United States government. Like any political movement, radical Islamism emphasizes the shaping of public opinion in the course of changing the political and constitutional orders of countries around the world. Radical Islamists are diverse in their theological and political ideologies – far from monolithic and at times in murderous conflict with one another.

The 1979 revolution in Iran and the rise of the Taliban militia in Afghanistan are representative examples of two different types of radical Islamism manifested into political power. Some movements have the stated goal of reestablishing a caliphate – a political system under the control of an ideological vanguard to govern populations in specific geographic territory.

Others have the goal of subverting or overthrowing established constitutional governments and use their politicized interpretations of the Qur'an as the basis of a new constitutional order, with Shar'ia as the law. This type of political system, formerly used by the Taliban and still the basis of the hard-line Wahhabi government of Saudi Arabia, takes a holy book that Muslims believe is divinely inspired, and turns it into a political manifesto of men and not God. In recognizing the regime of Saudi Arabia, the United States officially recognizes the political nature of the Qur'an as the Saudi constitution. Thus official U.S. policy already differentiates between the Qur'an as a theological document and as a political one.

Thus clerics and theologians who pursue political power must be regarded, for practical purposes, in their temporal roles as political leaders and operators. Such figures do not require the deference due to purely spiritual religious leaders.

Approaching radical Islamism as a political force can liberate American policymakers from the self-imposed, paralyzing angst that many suffer about the religious aspects of the conflict. This anxiety is as strong within the Department of Defense and uniformed services as anywhere else. It is a form of unilateral disarmament that gives the enemy more time, more insights into what we can and cannot do to them, ultimately more freedom of action, and aids their attrition campaign against us. It is the type of unilateral disarmament that gets our own forces, those of our allies, and innocent civilians senselessly maimed or killed.

Here at home, radical Islamists seek the overthrow of the Constitution of the United States. They may actively seek its destruction, or say simply that the Qur'an should replace it. Every U.S. government official – civilian and military – is legally bound to protect and defend the Constitution against such foreign and domestic enemies. Thus the need for something between public diplomacy and military force becomes more apparent as an immediate wartime tool. Such a tool can be applied precisely and decisively to reduce our reliance on the blunt instrument of military power.

Another artificial barrier that hinders the fight

The twin devil of our inability to fight the enemy as it should be fought is the defeatist interpretation of an obsolete law aimed against the legacy of President Franklin D. Roosevelt. That law is now invoked to prevent warfighters, diplomats and other government officials from running effective information campaigns against the enemy. A tiny clause of the U.S. Information and Educational

Exchange Act of 1948, known as the Smith-Mundt Act, forbids certain government officials and agencies from disseminating information in the U.S. that is intended for recipients abroad.

In fact, many legal and ethical ways exist to prevent Smith-Mundt disciples from shutting down effective messaging operations, even if Congress is unwilling to change the law. When the widespread use of the Internet showed policymakers that technology had made the old laws obsolete, the Clinton Administration found an easy way around the obstacle. Legally, and with no objection or challenge, the administration circumvented Smith-Mundt by hosting Voice of America websites on servers physically located in foreign countries. That precedent remains in force, but is not used as widely as it might be. Public affairs officers (PAOs) often veto military information operations (IO) designed to exploit terrorist websites, on the grounds that Arabic-speaking American citizens might see the U.S.-sponsored content and thus cause the military to be in violation of Smith-Mundt.

The executive branch should obtain a realistic legal opinion of the application of Smith-Mundt and its limitations. The administration must instruct PAOs to abide by the letter and spirit of the up-to-date legal interpretation. It must provide government-wide political support to give practitioners as much latitude as possible to do their hearts-and-minds work abroad. It must also ask Congress to modernize the law.

The necessity to follow these recommendations is simple and obvious. We cannot fight and win a war of ideas by denying ourselves the primary means of engaging this adversary and by muting our influence warriors. Not when our enemy uses these same tools so effectively to mobilize its support base, intimidate opponents and discredit and disparage us. We cannot concede this key terrain to our adversaries who then use it directly and indirectly to influence our domestic population, our politicians and our judges. We can and must contest this space. The enemy is already doing their best to deny these tools to us. We do not need to be complicit in this strategy.

Public diplomacy: building on – and breaking with – the traditional approach

The idea of public diplomacy and the official definition of the term have changed over time and often vary according to the perspectives of those who view the mission. At one end, it can be psychological and political warfare. On the other, it is passive "soft power."[3] Both tools are important, but neither is sufficient in itself.

Message warfare

The demise of the U.S. Information Agency and public diplomacy is well documented elsewhere, and a study group of The Institute of World Politics will make its own modalities proposal in a monograph to accompany this volume. Going back to our nation's roots, it becomes clear that scrappy, low-budget political warfare – attacking the target with negative messages, combining these attacks with overt and covert political organization and agitation, and offering positive alternatives – was a fundamental element of the American war of independence from Great Britain. These activities understandably carried a compelling sense of urgency about them.[4]

The U.S. has episodically waged such efforts internationally in support of its interests through the 19th and especially through much of the second half of the 20th century. Such strategies were not necessarily instinctive to diplomats or public diplomats, yet both recognized the need and knew how it integrated with their missions. After the National Security Act of 1947, a permanent government entity, the CIA, existed to provide the intellectual, legal, political and material tools to carry out covert political operations abroad.

---

[3] Joseph S. Nye, Jr., *Soft Power: The Means to Success in World Politics* (Public Affairs, 2004).

[4] For a discussion of American revolutionary public diplomacy and political warfare, see J. Michael Waller, "Public Diplomacy, Political Warfare and the American Tradition," in *Strategic Influence: Public Diplomacy, Counterpropaganda and Political Warfare* (The Institute of World Politics Press, 2007), Chapter One. Also see Gladys Thum and Marcella Thum, "War Propaganda and the American Revolution: The Pen and the Sword," in Garth S. Jowett and Victoria O'Donnell, eds., *Readings in Propaganda and Persuasion: New and Classic Essays* (Sage, 2006), pp. 73-82.

Those tools practically do not exist any more at the national strategic level.

Though the passage of time and changing attitudes to statecraft give it an almost archaic air, no other terms properly describe the third way between diplomacy and armed combat: political and psychological warfare. U.S. national security culture fostered careful study and practice of global psychological warfare strategy in order to resolve or win conflicts around the world without escalating to all-out war. President Truman created a Psychological Strategy Board under the National Security Council to plan, coordinate and approve global psychological operations. The U.S. has had nothing quite like it since.

Political warfare and psychological operations

Veteran practitioner and historian Wilson Dizard traces U.S. public diplomacy's origins to the Office of War Information of World War II, and unabashedly calls public diplomacy a function of ideological warfare.[5] Public diplomacy's tactical military cousin is psychological operations (PSYOP), a discipline that the Department of Defense defines as "Planned operations to convey selected information and indicators to foreign audiences to influence their emotions, motives, objective reasoning, and ultimately the behavior of foreign governments, organizations, groups, and individuals."[6]

"Hearts and minds," for want of a better term, refers specifically to the psyche. Yet we tend to run away from the true meaning as we try to rebuild our strategic communication capabilities.

A fighting spirit need not compromise the discipline's integrity as long as public diplomacy is a component of, instead of an umbrella for, a larger communication strategy. A 1989 National Defense University study offered an integrated view of how public diplomacy fits into the American defense arsenal:

> Public diplomacy is a form of international political advocacy directed openly by civilians to a broad spectrum of audiences. . . . It is aimed at civilians and is confined in the main to forms of advocacy available to host governments. It seeks to elicit popular

---

[5] Wilson P. Dizard, Jr., *Inventing Public Diplomacy: The Story of the U.S. Information Agency* (Lynne Reinner, 2004), pp. 2-3.
[6] *Department of Defense Dictionary of Military and Associated Terms*, Joint Pubs 1-02, 1994.

support for solutions of mutual benefit that avoids threats, compulsion, or intimidation. It is not a form of political warfare, although it may be used in combination with political warfare.[7]

Political warfare is the art and practice of waging and winning international conflicts by non-military means. Political warfare is explicitly aggressive and hostile in intent. Many public diplomacy practitioners are uneasy with or even hostile to the idea of strategic political warfare, as are many government public affairs professionals.

And for good reasons.[8] Credible public diplomacy depends on openness and trust, and strong firewalls to separate it from the tougher disciplines.[9] However, the reality of ideological conflict is its heavily psychological nature. But political warfare, like PSYOP, is an important, non-lethal weapon that can work where public diplomacy and other forms of communication cannot, and can complement or even substitute for military action. The nation's short-term messaging needs to call for a punchier approach.

Fighting on the psychological defensive

Waging a psychological form of siege warfare, some of the world's top terrorists and their supporters believe that their opponents will lose heart if the conflict is sufficiently drawn out. Since antiquity, militarily inferior forces successfully have drawn superior foes into a protracted conflict in a sound politico-military strategy. "Victory is the main object in war," ancient Chinese

---

[7] Paul A. Smith, *On Political War* (Washington: National Defense University Press, 1989), p. 7.

[8] Such unease is nothing new; even proponents of psychological warfare felt uneasy about the term when developing the discipline after World War II. Then, as now, many practitioners and policy professionals have trouble using the word "propaganda" to define influence activity, when as a neutral term propaganda is exactly what public diplomacy, political warfare and, for that matter, marketing and advertising, is all about.

[9] Building firewalls between public diplomacy, political warfare and other strategic communication while integrating each element is an ongoing subject of study and debate. See Bruce Gregory, "Public Diplomacy and Strategic Communication: Cultures, Firewalls and Imported Norms," paper presented to the American Political Science Association Conference on International Communication and Conflict, August 31, 2005.

military philosopher Sun Tzu warned in 500 B.C., adding, "If this is long delayed, weapons are blunted and morale depressed . . . When your weapons are dulled and ardour damped, your strength exhausted and treasure spent, neighboring rulers will take advantage of your distress to act."[10] Terrorists and insurgents can win by simply not losing. Governments and armies generally cannot.

Modern democratic societies are especially vulnerable to a highly motivated enemy that can manipulate public opinion and the perceptions of their leaders, and erode and break national will. Armed with a fanatical motivation that welcomes death, the extreme Islamist enemy is comfortable with the concept of diminishing the target's will to fight – not necessarily at the combatant level on the battlefront, but on the political level in the targeted societies. Indeed, most enemy combat operations are designed to achieve a political and psychological impact rather than an attritional or physical impact.

Captured al Qaeda manuals show that the radical Islamists have made careful studies of the writings of Mao, the campaigns of other Islamist terrorist organizations including Hizbollah, and the conduct of the Vietnam war. They perceive the Vietnam war as a classical case of how a militarily and politically inferior force can defeat a quantitatively and qualitatively superior force by undermining the will of that force's home population and political leadership. The U.S. military's new counterinsurgency doctrine emphasizes the political nature of the conflict and the Al Qaeda manuals and methods show natural expertise in manipulating images and emotions to exploit democratic policymaking processes in the United States and elsewhere.[11]

Al Qaeda leader confident that U.S. will lose the will to fight

The enemy's delivery system channels images and messages into the eyes and ears of the world public and especially those who make and shape policy and opinion. The enemy monitors American public opinion closely. Osama bin Laden explained this directly, addressing

---

[10] Sun Tzu, *The Art of War*, trans. Samuel B. Griffith, II:3-5.

[11] David E. Spencer, "Red-Teaming Political Warfare," in Waller, ed., *Strategic Influence*, op. cit. Spencer is a professor at the National Defense University.

the American public in a recording aired through Aljazeera in January, 2006:

> What prompted me to speak are the repeated fallacies of your President Bush in his comment on the outcome of the U.S. opinion polls, which indicated that the overwhelming majority of you want the withdrawal of the forces from Iraq, but he objected to this desire and said that the withdrawal of troops would send a wrong message to the enemy.

Bin Laden noted the daily roadside bombings in Iraq whose attrition of U.S. and coalition military personnel has become the greatest catalyst to the erosion of support for the war effort there. He attempted to draw parallels between U.S. soldiers in Iraq and Vietnam:

> The Pentagon figures indicate the rise in the number of your dead and wounded, let alone the huge material losses, and let alone the collapse of the morale of the soldiers there and the increase in the suicide cases among them.

> So, just imagine the state of psychological breakdown that afflicts the soldier while collecting the remnants of his comrades' dead bodies after they hit mines, which torn [sic] them. Following such [a] situation, the soldier becomes between two fires. If he refuses to go out of his military barracks for patrols, he will face the penalties of the Vietnam butcher, and if he goes out, he will face the danger of mines.

> So, he is between two bitter situations, something which puts him under psychological pressure – fear, humiliation, and coercion. Moreover, his people are careless about him. So he has no choice [but] to commit suicide.

While bin Laden missed the mark about the American soldiers' choices, he understands the effect of attrition campaigns. The al Qaeda leader focused not merely on the psychological effect of the roadside bombs on U.S. troops in Iraq, but on the American public back home. The results of American public opinion polls seemed to reinforce bin Laden's confidence: "To go back to where I started, I say that the results of the poll satisfy sane people that Bush's objection to them is false." A third time in the Aljazeera broadcast, bin Laden commented on "the substance of the results of opinion polls on withdrawing the troops" from Iraq.[12]

Bin Laden offered a truce and threatened similar terrorist campaigns in the United States. He hinted that the Americans lack the patience to win:

- "Do not be deluded by your power and modern weapons. Although they win some battles, they lose the war. Patience and steadfastness are better than them."
- ". . . we will take revenge . . . until your minds are exhausted and your lives become miserable."
- ". . . our situation is getting better, while your situation is getting worse."
- "We will remain patient in fighting you."[13]

Could the al Qaeda leader have a point about American resolve? Weeks after Aljazeera aired the bin Laden recording, a wealthy American antiwar activist commissioned a prominent polling company to survey the views of U.S. military personnel deployed inside Iraq. (Why U.S. commanders allowed the pollsters access to the troops is unclear.) The poll purportedly found that the majority of American troops in Iraq felt that the U.S. should pull out within 12 months, thus contradicting official government and Pentagon statements, and appearing to ratify bin Laden's analysis.[14]

The American psychological fatigue that the terrorist leader observed is indeed occurring. The quartet of suicide bombers, roadside bombs, TV and the Internet appear to be working well for the insurgents and terrorists. This is something that public diplomacy, by its long-term nature, is not intended to fix. So here is a vulnerability gap that needs to be closed and soon. We need to break the psychological siege not only by trying to win the wide middle of the undecided and softer opponents, but by directly attacking the enemy's own circles of support – and even the

---

[12] Osama bin Laden, "Text – Bin Laden Tape," BBC, January 19, 2006.
[13] Ibid.
[14] Al Pessin, "Poll Indicates U.S. Troops in Iraq Favor Withdrawal," Voice of America, March 1, 2006. The federally-funded LeMoyne College Center for Peace and Global Studies commissioned Zogby International to conduct the poll.

terrorists' cadres – on the intellectual and emotional fronts.[15] If we cannot get the enemy with kinetic actions, we can strike them with psychological weapons. Part of that means viewing television and the Internet as weapons – not merely for command and control or delivering munitions to targets, but as delivery systems to drop content on targets that we cannot physically locate.

Turn the tables: Bring the fight to the enemy

Here is where we ought to adapt traditional public diplomacy to current realities: to promote American ideas and ideals in a positive way, and also to bring the political and ideological fight to the enemy by using public diplomacy instruments and related resources as means of attack. This approach has many precedents since the American Revolution. Founding documents such as the Declaration of Independence offer a model: present uplifting goals and beliefs to take the moral high ground, and attack the enemy mercilessly. In the words of Samuel Adams, the message must always "keep the Enemy in the Wrong." The message-makers under Presidents Wilson, Roosevelt, Truman, Eisenhower, Kennedy and Reagan followed the Founders' model. They ably combined gentle and sometimes passive public diplomacy with political and psychological warfare to confront and attack, instead of merely defend against, the adversary's propaganda and ideological warfare.

Note the simple wartime message-making formula: a soft policy to tell the world of our intentions and what we stand for in positive and hopeful tones, in the appropriate linguistic and cultural settings, with the punch of a simultaneous strategic influence offensive to discredit and ultimately destroy the enemy as a political, moral and psychological force. Public diplomacy and strategic communications in general are thus back in balance. The tools now assume far more

---

[15] The 2006 *Counterinsurgency Field Manual* FM 3-24 stresses the need to split the enemy as an early order of business. By contrast, the Voice of America did not help the war effort in the way it covered the March 1 poll of troops in Iraq. The poll was the lead story on VOA's English-language online service, and VOA did not mention that a wealthy American antiwar activist paid for the survey until the last sentence of the 15-paragraph story. VOA did not cover comments by analysts across the American political spectrum who found fault with the poll's methodology.

vitality than mere auxiliaries for diplomatic support. They become strategic weapons.[16]

Subdue the enemy's will

If the war of ideas is a clash of wills, and human will is centered in the brain, then the target in this war is the mind. Politics, diplomacy and warfare all involve bending and at times breaking the will of an opponent. From a military perspective, the brain is therefore a legitimate military target. However, our traditional military approach has not been to influence that target, but to destroy it.

That might work in fast, short-term operations against known targets where persuasion is impossible or undesirable. But it can seldom produce desired results in a lengthy military occupation or a protracted conflict. For our purposes, rather than breaking hostile will by killing terrorists, we should find situations that produce equal or superior results through a larger concentration of politics and psychology. Many of our enemies are not mere inanimate entities requiring either our defeatist coexistence with them or their physical destruction. They are living beings with their own willpower that can be broken, subdued, or in many cases, positively influenced.

The situation will vary from country to country, within countries, and over time and circumstance. In Iraq, for example, we unwittingly turned people against us when they could have been our allies. A recent study of British military attitudes toward U.S. conduct in Iraq states:

> The lack of cultural awareness has prevented the Coalition from fully exploiting traditional and nontraditional leadership, tribal loyalties, and the Arab honor code in order to encourage the local population to isolate itself from the insurgents. The Coalition has also consistently failed to counter enemy propaganda, allowing the insurgents to promote themselves as the providers of hope, to discredit the Coalition, and to intimidate wavering communities.

---

[16] Strategic communications could assume a role as a peer to classical diplomacy and military power, much as the Bush administration has elevated foreign development and humanitarian assistance (on paper, at least) as pillars of national security. Such a role implies entirely new conceptual, structural and procedural changes that go beyond the scope of this monograph. The Defense Science Board has taken the lead in this area, with the State Department starting a strategy about two years later.

Coalition actions including the excessive use of force and indiscriminate and poorly targeted cordon-and-search operations have actually encouraged communities to embrace the terrorists, if not because of a belief in their cause, then for revenge.[17]

So how can we work to subdue the hostile will that we helped create? Col. Richard Szafranski USAF (Ret.), an early information warfare theoretician, argued more than a decade ago, "if the object of war truly is *to subdue hostile will or to make the opponent comply with our will*, then we must consider enemies not just as systems, but as organisms with will. Likewise, if weapons are *means used to coerce an adversary's will*, then our understanding of weapons must go beyond tangible things, implements or tools."[18] As a battlefield commander in World War II, Dwight D. Eisenhower intimately understood the power of psychological warfare to undermine an enemy's morale and actively supported the development of a robust U.S. Army PSYOP capability. As president early in the Cold War, Eisenhower took the military psychological skills he developed against the Nazis and applied them as a civilian leader against the Soviet Union and communism, taking the fight to the enemy in every corner of the planet.[19]

The emphasis today, though, has been on subduing and destroying the will's host – the adversary's physical brain – instead of subduing the will itself, which is governed by the mind that resides in the neocortex. Szrafranski continues:

> Because we believe that the entity 'will' is existential and brain-centered, we concentrate our attention on the existence of brains, not on the nature of will. In so doing we may have mistakenly identified the *craft* of war as the *art* of war. By that I mean that our science of

---

[17] See Andrew Garfield, *Succeeding in Phase IV: British Perspectives on the U.S. Effort to Stabilize and Reconstruct Iraq* (Foreign Policy Research Institute/GlobalSecurityMedia, 2006).

[18] Richard Szafranski, "Neocortical Warfare? The Acme of Skill," *Military Review*, November 1994, pp. 41-55. Reprinted in John Arquilla and David Ronfeldt, eds., *In Athena's Camp: Preparing for Conflict in the Information Age* (RAND Corporation, 1997), pp. 395-416. Emphasis in original.

[19] See Blanche Wiesen Cook, *The Declassified Eisenhower: A Divided Legacy of Peace and Political Warfare* (Doubleday, 1981); and Kenneth Osgood, *Total Cold War: Eisenhower's Secret Propaganda Battle at Home and Abroad* (University of Kansas Press, 2006).

war is not so much the study of subduing will as it is the means of devising and applying progressively more elaborate means and methods for destroying brains. Destroy enough brains, or the correct brains, our studies seem to encourage us, and 'will' necessarily dies along with the organism.

That approach arguably has encouraged the overkill that our British allies worry about.[20] In a prolonged conflict it appears to be militarily unsound. With huge communication resources, it is usually immoral. The 2006 *Counterinsurgency Field Manual*, which lays out a revolutionary change in military doctrine, recognizes those concerns, advising that at times, "the more force is used, the less effective it is," and that "some of the best weapons for counterinsurgents do not shoot."[21]

Peeling the onion

We create deadly problems for ourselves when our nation's actions unite people against us. When they unite extremist factions that direct their violence away from each other and at our own forces, the problem is far worse. So our message strategy must be designed to be as divisive to our foes as possible.

We can compare the physical universe of opposition to an onion: a three-dimensional, roughly spherical universe consisting of concentric layers. At the center is the hard core of the most intransigent opposition. At the outermost layers, the opposition is the weakest. Our divisive strategy is to peel away the outer layers of opposition, getting down as close to the core as possible with a minimum of lethal force. Each layer we peel away is a layer that no longer identifies with the enemy and starts to realize it has a vested future in our success. The closer we get to the hard core, the more difficult it is to peel away the most benighted layers of hard-core activists and terrorists or insurgents. At that point the use of military power becomes necessary, accepted and effective.

It is here that our attempts to divide will be the most challenging. They might also be the most important, as they will focus on breaking up personal networks and provoking resentments, suspicions, fear and paranoia, and ultimately generating betrayals

---

[20] Garfield, op. cit.
[21] *Counterinsurgency Field Manual* 3-24, pp. 1-150, 1-152 and 1-153.

and defections, allowing the U.S. to identify and destroy the most intransigent targets.

The layered-onion metaphor presents a challenge to advocates of democratization. We are attempting, as we peel away layers, to win anti-democratic and very hostile elements away from the hard core. We are not trying to persuade them of the virtues of democracy, the liberation of women, or alternate lifestyles. We are not necessarily trying to make them our friends. We don't expect expressions of gratitude. We are simply appealing to their own interests as the enemy of their enemy.

Once we establish the enemy-of-your-enemy relationship, we will succeed in reducing hostility against us and allow us to form some sort of temporary alliance or working relationship. That uncomfortable alliance of convenience, for the short-term, will be sufficient to help us isolate and subdue the most intransigent. Over the long-term we will have to keep splitting, isolating and destroying the successively most extreme remaining elements while avoiding radicalization of the healthy outer layers. Historically we have often succeeded with this strategy when we applied it in counter-insurgency. (We will return to the onion metaphor in Chapter 6 to discuss the variegated messages to use when splitting the opposition.)

Immediate-term approach: Messages on two fronts

We can summarize traditional public diplomacy's message-making approach with the following basic themes:

- tell America's story;
- engage in dialogue (not monologue) with the rest of the world;
- resolve misunderstandings;
- build international relationships; and
- work together in a spirit of friendship and common purpose.

Shorter-term approaches must be calculated:

- to divide our opposition, wherever it is, even of and within our traditional allies in the industrialized democracies;
- isolate the enemy;
- coerce and subdue hostile will; and
- ultimately eliminate those who would do harm.

Note the important distinctions between "opposition" or "adversary" on the one hand, and "enemy" on the other. Our opposition and even adversary might be a normally close ally or important partner. It need not be a belligerent. The opposition or adversary could be a legitimate, mainstream political party or politician in a given country. Even so, the persuasion component directed at an adversary must be part of a counterterrorist or counterinsurgency strategy.

We can illustrate the new approach as a stylized addition formula, showing how the traditional public diplomacy approaches in the left column, plus the wartime accelerant on the right, add up in the war of ideas:

Public diplomacy		**Added accelerant**
Long-term relationships	+	*Immediate-term needs*
Promote our image	+	*Attack enemy's image*
Tell our story	+	*Discredit enemy's story*
Engage in dialogue	+	*Take control of language*
Discuss differences	+	*Discuss common enemy*
Resolve misunderstandings	+	*Reach proper understandings*
Build relationships	+	*Divide critics and foes*
Raise hope and morale	+	*Break hostile will*
Become friends	+	*Become 'enemy of enemy'*
Cooperate (as friends)	+	*Collaborate (as allies)*

This dual approach is the heart of an immediate wartime message strategy. Its development and implementation require no legislation or bureaucratic reorganizations. With a simple directive, the president can create an interagency task force and appoint and empower his own staff to call and run the meetings and ensure the compliance of all relevant agencies. Strong and successful precedent exists for such an entity.[22]

Conclusion

Deployment of a simple immediate-term message strategy will accelerate the shaping of international perceptions, opinions and behavior about the United States and its enemies for wartime purposes. It must combine the positive vision and soft approach of traditional public diplomacy with an assertive and relentless political and psychological campaign designed to subdue the enemy's will and prevent others from developing the will to terrorize, while providing optimism and developmental and economic assistance to sustain and build morale at home and abroad.

The immediate strategy provides the intellectual and political spadework toward building a new, more energetic and more creative public diplomacy and strategic communication system. This system anticipates rather than reacts. When it must be reactive, it is dynamic and flexible. It accepts a diversity of new approaches and functions. And it is opportunity-oriented to take immediate advantage of rapidly changing situations.

---

[22] The Reagan Administration's public diplomacy coordination model is a useful example, as formed by National Security Decision Directive 77, "Management of Public Diplomacy Relative to National Security," January 14, 1983. For a first-person account of the success of the Reagan interagency working group to counter Soviet active measures, see Herbert Romerstein, "The Interagency Active Measures Working Group: An eyewitness account of the U.S. government's confrontation of Soviet disinformation," in Waller, ed., *Strategic Influence*, op. cit.

2

The importance of words

Introduction

Words and images are the most powerful weapons in a war of
ideas. Used skillfully, they can serve the cause well. Used carelessly,
they cause collateral damage and the equivalent of death by friendly
fire. Effective messages require understanding, development and
deployment of the proper words – not only as Americans understand
them in English, but as the rest of the world understands them in
many cultural contexts and languages.

Message-making requires sophisticated understanding of both
friend and enemy. It requires confident self-knowledge. It requires
instinct and an intimate understanding about how information is
disseminated today. Most of all, successful message-making requires
personal courage against critics abroad and at home. Inexpert or
timid use of words undermines the mission and inadvertently aids
the enemy every bit as much as the military indiscipline that made
Abu Ghraib a metaphor to many for America's presence in Iraq.

In this chapter we discuss:

- how words are used as instruments of conflict and weapons of
  warfare;
- how the meanings of words differ among languages and
  cultures, and often within the same language and culture;
- how the nation's adversaries and enemies have used our own
  understandings of words against us, and how we accepted
  those hostile definitions as our own; and
- how we can take the language back from the enemy and make
  it work for the wartime and long-term interests of a civilized
  society.

Words as weapons

The human mind is the battlespace of the war of ideas. Words and images shape that battlespace. They create, define and elaborate ideas, and they can popularize or destroy the ideas' appeal. Messages require relentless repetition. Words are not static objects. The written and spoken word, as George Orwell said, can be used "as an instrument which we shape for our own purposes." In his famous essay "Politics and the English Language," Orwell explained the relationship between language and how people think: "if thought corrupts language, language can also corrupt thought. A bad usage can spread by tradition and imitation, even among people who should and do know better."[23]

Deliberate and unwitting corruption of language and thought applies as much to law, literature, love, marketing and politics as it does to diplomacy and warfare. Men have been using words to fight wars since the beginning of recorded history. Like iron, words can be forged from plowshares into swords and back again. Thucydides, in his monumental history of the Peloponnesian Wars, noted how the upturning of society during the Corcyrean civil war of 427 B.C. was paralleled by distortion of language on the part of the combatants:

> To fit in with the change of events, words, too, had to change their usual meanings. What used to be described as a thoughtless act of aggression was now regarded as the courage one would expect to find in a party member; to think of the future and wait was merely another way of saying one was a coward; any idea of moderation was just an attempt to disguise one's unmanly character; ability to understand a question from all sides meant that one was totally unfitted for action. Fanatical enthusiasm was the mark of a real man. . . .[24]

In this conflict, terms of moral judgment regularly described actions and events wholly alien to their true meanings, so that men

---

[23] George Orwell, "Politics and the English Language," in Sonia Orwell and Ian Angus, eds., *George Orwell: In Front of Your Nose, 1946-1950*, Vol. 4 (Boston: Nonpareil Books, 2002), pp. 127-140.

[24] Thucydides, *History of the Peloponnesian War*, 3.82[.4], trans. Rex Warner (Penguin, 1954, 1972). Richard Crowley translates 3.82.4 as, "Words had to change their ordinary meaning and to take that which was now given them."

could better justify deeds that would have been deemed reprehensible in times of peace. The chaos that resulted from the devious political manipulation of words did much to exacerbate the conflict and serves an early example of the power of rhetoric in politics, diplomacy and warfare.

Niccolò Machiavelli, the 15th century Florentine political philosopher and strategist, revolutionized statecraft in the western Christian world with his cynical, often amoral guidebook *The Prince*. His plays on words, invented definitions and purposeful distortions of language were part of his craft. Yet most translators of his works, according to Angelo Codevilla of Boston University, attempted to fix what they saw as Machiavelli's errors of syntax and usage, and inadvertently denied readers of English an accurate understanding of the use of words as weapons. Codevilla has translated *The Prince* with as faithful a preservation possible of Machiavelli's word games, making heavy annotations throughout. The result is a spicier if less smooth-sounding translation that offers a deeper understanding of Machiavelli's devious mind.[25]

The idealistic architects of American independence two-and-a-half centuries after Machiavelli saw word meanings change with their own ideas. They viewed themselves as patriotic Englishmen living in America, loyal to king and empire. Men like George Washington fought the French and Indian War (known in Europe as the Seven Years' War, but among some colonists as King George's War) as American Englishmen. Their grievance was that in America, the crown was denying them their rights as the king's subjects.

By 1769, Samuel Adams in Boston began successfully changing public opinion so that the loyal English patriot in America seeking his just rights was now an American patriot. One by one, over the years, other colonial leaders underwent the same transformation. Words and political organization were Adams' sole weapons, and the incendiary political strategist used them well. More than most, Adams recognized and worried about the enemy's distortion of language: "How strangely will the Tools of a Tyrant pervert the

---

[25] Niccolò Machiavelli, *The Prince*, trans. Angelo Codevilla (Yale University Press, 1997).

plain Meaning of Words!"[26] Adams, Benjamin Franklin, Thomas Paine and others made words suit their own meanings as well.

Free people must safeguard their languages and jealously protect the true meanings of words. Czechoslovakian President Václav Havel, just as the Soviet bloc was collapsing in 1989, warned the Western democracies about words and their double-edged power to corrode and demoralize the good. "Alongside words that electrify society with their freedom and truthfulness, we have words that mesmerize, deceive, inflame, madden, beguile, words that are harmful – lethal even," Havel said. Giving example after example, the former political prisoner-playwright-turned-president noted, "The same word can, at one moment, radiate great hope; at another, it can emit lethal rays. The same word can be true at one moment and false the next, at one moment illuminating, at another deceptive."[27]

Havel's strongest example was the word *peace*: "For forty years, an allergy to that beautiful word has been engendered in me, as it has in every one of my fellow citizens, because I know what the word has meant here for all those forty years: ever mightier armies ostensibly to defend peace."[28]

Semantics and rhetoric

Semantics, derived from the Greek *semantikos*, for "significant" or "significant meaning," is "the branch of linguistics and logic concerned with meaning," according to the *Oxford English Dictionary*. *Webster* gives semantics a more operational definition: "the language used (as in advertising or political propaganda) to achieve a desired effect on an audience especially through the use of words with novel or dual meanings." The first cousin of semantics is rhetoric, the ancient art of using expression and language effectively to persuade.

---

[26] Alexander, p. 74; Samuel Adams, letter to John Pitts, January 21, 1776, in Harry Alonzo Cushing, ed., *The Writings of Samuel Adams*, Vol. III (G.P. Putnam's Sons, 1904-1908; Gutenberg Project eText 2093, 1999).

[27] Václav Havel, "A Word About Words," *in absentia* speech, Frankfurt, Germany, October 15, 1989, trans. A. G. Brain, published in the *New York Review of Books*, January 18, 1990. The text in English appears on Havel's homepage at: www.vaclavhavel.cz/index.php?sec=2&id=1 .

[28] Ibid.

Even Aristotle, who produced the first systematic treatment of rhetoric and invented the idea of logic, saw the dark side of the art as well as the bright. To Aristotle, rhetoric consisted of three "proofs" of persuasion: *logos* (words), *ethos* (character of the speaker), and *pathos* (the psychological element).[29] A competent rhetorician could argue through the use of words in a logical form to move popular passion, explain complicated ideas simply, whip up emotions and calm down hatred and fear. Aristotle discussed how rhetoric fits in a democratic society. He seemed torn by his own idea. Among his concerns about the use of rhetoric was the danger that in the hands of the wrong people, the art could be a destructive weapon. We can conclude from Aristotle that, like any armament, rhetoric is a danger when used by the enemy, and, when used carelessly, by ourselves. Democratic forces must not be unilaterally disarmed. They must be thoroughly trained, enculturated and mobilized to be as adept with words as they are with precision munitions.

Unfortunately, the reality is that many Americans in government have lost the art of rhetoric as an instrument of statecraft, though most of the Founding Fathers, including Samuel Adams, were students of Aristotle. Sixty years ago Orwell saw a sharp decline in the skillful use of language among English-speaking politicians and journalists. He warned after World War II that if the trend continued, the societies and leaders of the English-speaking world would find that poor use of language would corrupt their thought processes and alter their perceptions of their own civilizations. Critics of today's political correctness movement would agree.

Twenty-first century Americans have demonstrated little ability or inclination to use language effectively in the war of ideas abroad, showing much greater facility and ease with destroying fellow human beings physically as a first option, instead of trying to "destroy" the pernicious ideologies that motivate their hostile will. Yet they use semantics and rhetoric instinctively and skillfully in fighting political wars against one another at home, with politicians of all stripes routinely using military jargon in their civil discourse

---

[29] Aristotle, *On Rhetoric*, trans. George A. Kennedy (Oxford University Press, 1991); and Aristotle, *The Art of Rhetoric*, trans. H. C. Lawson-Tancred (Penguin, 1991). Also see Aristotle, *The Politics*, trans. Carnes Lord (University of Chicago Press, 1984).

and action.[30] We can see how the political lines are drawn about any one issue by picking out the wording that a faction consciously or unconsciously uses. Each side employs idealistic or distorted language to promote its own views while demonizing or otherwise de-legitimizing the positions of the other.[31]

Complications of culture

Cross-linguistic and cross-cultural factors complicate semantics and rhetoric, especially where there is no *Webster's* to standardize definitions, and where meaning is in the beholder's mind. To demonstrate how even some of the most successful communicators can fail by misunderstanding semantics, many marketing texts, seminars and websites point to a disastrous snafu that General Motors is said to have made in the 1960s when it sold one of its most successful U.S. models, the Chevrolet Nova, in Latin America. To a Spanish-speaker, some textbooks say, the English word "Nova" sounds similar to the Spanish expression *no va*, which means "doesn't go." Understandably, despite a reversed syllabic order, the unintended slogan "Chevy won't go" helped explain the car's poor regional sales and why GM changed the name for Spanish-speaking markets.[32]

---

[30] See John J. Pitney, Jr., *The Art of Political Warfare* (Norman: University of Oklahoma Press/Red River, 2000).

[31] Depending on one's political or philosophical views today, a controversial public program is paid either with "government funding" or "taxpayer dollars," i.e., money that is either property of the government (and therefore nobly "invested"), or the fruits of the work of the people (a waste of people's hard-earned money). Congress either "taxes the rich" (good, according to some) or "penalizes the most successful" (bad for those who work hard). The abortion debate is loaded with the labels "pro-choice" or "pro-abortion" on one side, depending on who is doing the labeling, and "pro-life," "anti-abortion," or "anti-choice" on the other. Each side views the subject through completely unrelated frames of reference. Other examples in current usage: Illegal aliens (pejorative) or undocumented immigrants (euphemistic); prostitutes (once neutral and mainstream) or sex workers (newly legitimizing); liberal (often pejorative) or progressive (euphemistic); right-wing (usually pejorative) or conservative (euphemistic).

[32] "Naming Products Is No Game," *Business Week*, April 9, 2004.

Or so the storytellers said. The tale is an urban legend. The Chevy Nova, in fact, sold well in Latin America as the Nova. In trying to show how ignorant the world's largest automaker could be despite its army of Spanish-speaking marketers and dealers, the legend's purveyors and believers display their own lack of cultural awareness. They presume that English words and phrases have exactly the same meaning when translated literally to or from other languages.

The Nova/*no va* blunder simply does not translate. Cars might "go" in English, but not in Spanish. Depending on regional word usage and the age of the speaker, automobiles "walk" (*caminar*), "march" (*marchar*), "function" (*funcionar*) or "serve" (*servir*). Automobiles that "run" and "go" can sound as absurd to the native speaker of Spanish as "walking" and "marching" cars sound to the native English speaker.[33]

The entirety of the Nova myth, from the false story itself to its almost unquestioned repetition, illustrates how misunderstanding of even the most familiar foreign languages and cultures can affect our perceptions of the rest of the world. Misunderstanding affects how we see other peoples and as we attempt to deliver messages to change perceptions, attitudes and behavior abroad.[34]

Our main sources of public information – political leaders and journalists – use foreign words and expressions in their own daily written and verbal communication, and inject them into public discourse. Satisfied with popular usage or *Webster's* American English definition (which under normal circumstances would be sufficient), few double-check with linguists or scholars about the precise or varied meanings, and many occasionally repeat "new" words, readily accepting them at face value without regard to the source, and pass them and the distortions of their meanings on to the public and key decision makers.

Those distortions, a form of shorthand that become unprovable "known facts," affect the new users' perceptions and can adversely

---

[33] See Brian Akre, "Chevy's 'No-va' and Other Durable Urban Legends," *General Motors FYI Blog*, April 24, 2006; and Barbara and David Mikkelson, "Don't Go Here," Snopes.com, updated February 19, 2007.

[34] While the Chevy Nova story is false, Mitsubishi found that it had to change the name of its popular Pajero SUV for sales in the Americas and Spain, where the vehicle is known as the Montero, or "mountaineer." To many speakers of Spanish, "pajero" is vulgar slang for a self-gratifying male. See "Naming Products Is No Game," *Business Week*, op. cit.

influence policy. Unquestioned acceptance or repetition of the distorted words can cause fundamental misunderstandings, and not only at home. By their cumulative repetition in the press and in public statements they can be politically or diplomatically damaging abroad as well.

Defensive mechanism

We in the United States have no institutional defense against our own misinterpretations of true meanings, or against the conscious efforts of adversaries to induce or reinforce our own misunderstandings. Concerned about the problem during the heated years of the Cold War, the U.S. Advisory Commission on Public Diplomacy reported:

> We believe that the times require a conscious effort to improve the accuracy and political impact of words and terms used by our leaders in speaking to the world. By so doing, they can help disclose the hypocrisy and distortions of hostile propaganda. This is not a problem that will go away, and we must be prepared to deal with it on a systematic and continuing basis.

The commissioners recommended:

> that a task force be created, under the National Security Council and including representatives of the Departments of State and Defense and USIA [U.S. Information Agency], to assess the problem and propose an institutionalized means to respond to inaccurate or misleading terminology in international political discourse.[35]

The recommendation was not to form a task force to counter disinformation; the White House National Security Council already had an interagency working group and USIA had established a new office for that purpose.[36] The task force would not craft positive

---

[35] Edwin J. Feulner, Jr., Chairman, United States Advisory Commission on Public Diplomacy, *The Role of USIA and Public Diplomacy*, January 1984.
[36] "Disinformation" refers to the deliberate fabrication and circulation of false facts. The USIA unit was the two-man Office to Counter Soviet Disinformation and Active Measures, which existed from 1983 to 1989. Its former director, Herbert Romerstein, authored a chapter on counterpropaganda in *Strategic Influence*, op. cit.

messages about the United States, which was one of the decades-long public diplomacy missions of the USIA as a whole. The commissioners were referring specifically to words and terms that, through misuse or abuse, became assets of the enemy by altering how we perceive, think and act.

Semantic infiltration

A war of ideas is well-fought when a skilled or persistent semanticist can persuade an opponent to accept his terms of debate, especially when the words are those that form the ideas that motivate the will. The opponent thus unwittingly through repetition or willingly through persuasion adopts the semanticist's usage of words and by extension, the ideas, perceptions and policies that accompany them. Fred Charles Iklé, in a 1970s Rand Corporation study on the difficulties the United States faced in negotiating with Communist regimes, called the phenomenon "semantic infiltration." According to Iklé:

> Paradoxically, despite the fact that the State Department and other government agencies bestow so much care on the vast verbal output of Communist governments, we have been careless in adopting the language of our opponents and their definitions of conflict issues in many cases where this is clearly to our disadvantage.

> Or perhaps this is not so paradoxical. It might be precisely because our officials spend so much time on the opponents' rhetoric that they eventually use his words – first in quotation marks, later without.[37]

Commenting on Iklé's paper, the late Senator Daniel Patrick Moynihan called semantic infiltration "the systematic distortion of the meaning of certain words to confuse or mislead." Semantic infiltration, said Moynihan,

> is the process whereby we come to adopt the language of our adversaries in describing political reality. The most brutal totalitarian regimes in the world call themselves 'liberation

---

[37] Fred Charles Iklé, cited in Daniel Patrick Moynihan, "Further Thoughts on Words and Foreign Policy," *Policy Review*, Spring 1979.

movements.' It is perfectly predictable that they should misuse words to conceal their real nature. But must we aid them in that effort by repeating those words? Worse, do we begin to influence our own perceptions by using them? [38]

By adopting communist labels, the senator and former U.N. ambassador argued, the State Department bought into the enemy's rhetoric and adversely affected U.S. attitudes toward a particular conflict. In Moynihan's words:

> Even though the State Department proclaimed its neutrality in the conflict there, its very choice of words – its use of the vocabulary of groups opposed to our values – undermined the legitimacy of the pro-Western political forces in the area. We pay for small concessions at the level of language with large setbacks at the level of practical politics. [39]

That "totalitarians will seek to seize control of the language of politics is obvious; that our own foreign affairs establishment should remain blind to what is happening is dangerous," Moynihan said. Soft-line foreign service officers weren't the only culprits. Even some of the staunchest hard-liners proved susceptible in Moynihan's time, as they can today, to semantic infiltration.

The worst totalitarians of Moynihan's time, the Soviets, mastered the use of semantics in political warfare. They corrupted positive words like "democratic," "fraternal," "liberation," "progressive," and "people." As Havel noted, they did the same with the idea of "peace." They then applied their corrupt meanings to totalitarian and terrorist regimes and movements. [40]

It was as if the West had stopped believing in its own values. American officials often shied away from using those words in defense of U.S. policy. Worse, they sometimes applied them in ways that benefited Soviet propaganda. They even were reluctant to turn Soviet jargon against Moscow, shying away from calling the USSR a dictatorship or empire. "Soviet imperialism" was almost never a

---

[38] Moynihan, Ibid., p. 53.

[39] Ibid.

[40] See Georgi Arbatov, *The War of Ideas in Contemporary International Relations* (Moscow, USSR: Progress Publishers, 1973); and Graham D. Vernon, ed., *Soviet Perceptions of War and Peace* (Washington: National Defense University Press, 1981).

term of U.S. public diplomacy; the State Department ceded the words – and thus the ideas – to the politburo to dominate.

For example, many in the American media and politics referred to Soviet-backed terrorist and guerrilla groups as "liberation movements," idealistic and selfless manifestations of oppressed peoples' democratic aspirations. Radical protests in Europe against the U.S. and NATO were led by "peace activists," when in reality they were always anti-American and never anti-Soviet, under the influence or control of the KGB and Soviet-controlled fronts.[41] Some Americans denounced their government's efforts to halt Soviet expansionism as "American imperialism," a made-in-Moscow epithet that has long outlived the USSR. Few in the mainstream ever referred to Soviet expansionism in an imperialistic light until after the Soviet collapse in 1991.[42]

Meanwhile, the Soviets raged against American "imperialism" while U.S. officials cringed and sneered at calling the USSR an empire, even after their president called it just that. Though few really believed that the Soviets were committed to "peace," these critics considered the U.S. and NATO the more clear and present dangers. Most of the world completely accepted and unwittingly helped to spread misleading communist jargon like "German Democratic Republic" and "People's Republic of China," validating totalitarian propaganda that suggested these regimes were democratic republics of the people.

Indeed, during the Cold War, Soviet use of peace propaganda had made many in the West so cynical that those who understood the Soviet danger best, from the center-left Havel to Reaganite conservatives, had difficulty using the word "peace" constructively

---

[41] Vladimir Bukovsky, "The Peace Movement and the Soviet Union," *Commentary*, May 1982; and U.S. Information Agency, *Soviet Active Measures in the 'Post-Cold War Era,' 1988-1991* (Report for the Committee on Appropriations of the U.S. House of Representatives, June 1992). In the early 1980s, some of Europe's ruling socialist parties, such as the SPD of West Germany, explicitly wanted the U.S. to deploy Pershing II intermediate-range nuclear ballistic missiles on their territory to counter the Soviets.

[42] Not that some didn't try. Hugh Seton-Watson's *The New Imperialism* (Dufor Editions, 1961) is an example. The bitter controversy surrounding President Ronald Reagan's 1983 denunciation of the Soviet Union as an "evil empire" shows how unacceptable such truth-telling was even in the Cold War's tense final years.

or even with a straight face. Such was the noxiousness of Soviet political warfare: civilized society lost control of the ideas that peace animated, and the Soviets hijacked naïve western hopes and fears by infiltrating, funding and manipulating the peace movements in the democracies. Those in the West who exposed such manipulation often faced derision and ridicule.

Those who saw through the propaganda were usually ideologically hostile to the Soviets and communism. However, they generally responded not by taking back the word but by declaring the "peace" movement to be nothing more than a sham of dupes and fools, hippies and sellouts. Some proudly proclaimed their militancy against the Soviet threat with statements and actions that reasonable but ill-informed people could perceive as being truly anti-peace. Until a communicator like Reagan arrived to lead, many anti-Soviet intellectuals used rhetoric and policies that alarmed the soft middle-of-the-roaders who found the KGB line so soothing.

In his speech, Havel noted the difference: "The same word can be humble at one moment and arrogant the next. And a humble word can be transformed easily and imperceptibly into an arrogant one, whereas it is a difficult and protracted process to transform an arrogant word into one that is humble."[43]

Welcome others' definition – and lose the language

Most Americans like, or at least fully accept, the idea that their nation is a superpower. The word was not invented as a compliment. The late Chinese communist leader Chou En-lai coined the term "superpower" pejoratively against the USSR and the United States. He did so in a 1970 interview with French journalists, as part of an effort to show developing nations a third way between America and the Soviet bloc. The name stuck.[44]

Both the Soviets and the Americans identified with the term and applied it proudly to themselves. But even though U.S. allies expressed satisfaction with a superpower protector, the idea helped crystallize fear and resentment around the world – sentiments that remain against the United States and complicate the current war effort. The term also helped solidify a global attitude of moral

---

[43] Havel, op. cit.

[44] Daniel Patrick Moynihan, "Further Thoughts on Words and Foreign Policy," *Policy Review*, Spring 1979, p. 57.

equivalence between the U.S. and the USSR.[45] Today, as "the world's only superpower," the U.S. has a new perception problem.

The easy, unchallenged acceptance of the adversaries' terms of debate showed a lack of national confidence and conviction, almost an admission that we thought we were on the losing side of history. It appeared to show abandonment in some quarters of the exceptionalism that had given the U.S. its moral standing in the world. Many Americans – shapers of opinion and policy among them – actually believed it, resigning the world to permanent "peaceful coexistence," at best, with the USSR, and rejecting as dangerous the idea that the U.S. could nudge the decayed and overextended Soviet system to collapse from within.[46] The peaceful coexistence and détente advocates made the defeatist temptation all the more difficult to resist.

Some recognized the problem and tried to change it. Early in his presidency, Ronald Reagan issued a secret National Security Decision Directive on relations with the USSR that outlined his strategy for confronting Moscow. In that document, known as NSDD-77, Reagan stated that United States policy would seek to "prevent the Soviet propaganda machine from seizing the semantic high-ground in the battle of ideas through the appropriation of such terms as 'peace.'" Even more, the president set an official policy to put the Soviets on the defensive, among other things, to "expose at all available *fora* the double standards employed by the Soviet Union within its own domain and the outside ('capitalist') world (e.g., treatment of labor, policies toward ethnic minorities, use of chemical weapons, etc.)."[47] The United States would finally take the world stage to attack the USSR at its weakest political points.

---

[45] At home, seeking convenient labels as shorthand to explain foreign issues to a domestic audience, the prestige press routinely and inaccurately referred to the KGB as the Russian "equivalent" to the FBI at home and CIA abroad, as if it was a legitimate law enforcement and intelligence service. And so on.

[46] The Reagan administration laid out the strategy to bring down the Soviet Union, as one of the architects, Norman Bailey, describes in his monograph. Norman A. Bailey, *The Strategic Plan that Won the Cold War – National Security Decision Directive 75* (Potomac Foundation, 1998).

[47] Ronald Reagan, "U.S. Relations with the USSR," National Security Decision Directive No. 75, January 17, 1983.

Inattention

For three years in a row, the Advisory Commission on Public Diplomacy under Edwin Feulner repeated its recommendation, in vain, to institutionalize a means to challenge inaccurate or misleading terminology. The government ignored it. Then came the Soviet collapse. The United States entered into a period of drift and withdrawal in the early 1990s. When faced with a new enemy, U.S. leaders found themselves groping for the right words in the new war of ideas, wondering, without a USIA and other services, why it was so difficult to get the world to support or understand our cause.

"The costs of inattention seem to escape even those among us who pride ourselves on their 'hardheadedness' in matters of geopolitics and military strategy," Moynihan wrote. Neither political party was immune: "This is not a phenomenon of one administration, but almost, I think, of our political culture."[48] The words, written in 1979, could have been written today. The more receptive the United States and the world become to enemy terminology, Moynihan warned, "the more will the nations of the world begin to accommodate themselves" to the adversary's strategic aspirations.[49]

And so it is today in the "Global War on Terror," not only among Americans or in the West, but in the ummah, the global community or nation of Islam itself. In the next chapter, we explore how words from the Arabic language and Islamic culture are used and abused, how semantic infiltration has warped the United States' understanding of key Muslim concepts, how that misunderstanding worldwide has allowed extremists to dominate language and ideas in Islam, and what the forces of civilization can do about it.

Conclusion

Knowing and dominating the definitions of words, cross-culturally, is key to winning the international war of ideas.

Public diplomacy, public affairs, information operations, psychological operations and political warfare are all aspects of strategic communication and counterinsurgency. They will be more effective if their practitioners fearlessly exploit the wealth of words that culture offers to define ideas and shape understanding of them.

---

[48] Ibid., pp. 58-59.
[49] Ibid., p. 55.

Those practitioners must lead: not at merely the presidential level or cabinet level, but at every level in the bureaucracy of every government agency involved with communication. They need not wait for bureaucratic reorganizations, legal reviews and congressional appropriations cycles. Fundamental shifts can begin with a single speech and skillful follow-up work. Successful shifts require leadership and relentless repetition at all levels. But the war of ideas will continue to suffer setbacks as long as those at the top continue to misunderstand or abuse words without regard for their best meanings.

3

Making *jihad* work for America

Introduction

How great it would be if we could use Arabic words and Muslim terms to denounce the terrorists as sociopaths instead of holy warriors. As waging an unholy war on innocent society instead of fighting the good fight for God. As murderers instead of martyrs. As plagues that must be wiped out – and preferably by their own people.

The good news is that we can. Best of all, Muslims and speakers of Arabic across the ideological spectrum traditionally accept the terminology as we would like it to mean. We just need to embrace and promote the words in our own discourse and messages.

In this chapter, we will look at how the U.S. and many of its allies misunderstand and misuse Islamic terminology, and how they may fix the problem quickly. Specifically, we will examine how Western societies fell victim to semantic infiltration. As a result, they:

- unwittingly framed the conflict of ideas on the enemy's terms;
- undermined "moderate" Muslims who oppose and fear the extremists;
- wrote off conservative Muslim traditionalists and fundamentalists as lost to the enemy camp, when in fact they have proven to be important allies;
- effectively declared that all practitioners of *jihad* – and not merely the extremists who had hijacked the word – were the sworn enemies of the United States;
- appeared to make the U.S. and other Western countries to be declaring war against Islam, even as they took pains to stress that they were not;

- reinforced many Muslims' predisposition to distrust the United States;
- validated the enemy's ideological worldview against the U.S. and the West;
- affirmed the enemy's sense of divine justice that drives people to murder and to destroy their own lives in the process;
- "branded" the enemy leadership, enhancing their reputations among those who would oppose us, and inspiring more recruits to their cause;
- sent the world a message that we don't know what we're doing;
- validated false suspicions about American motives;
- helped unite the Muslim opposition – and broaden and deepen it – against the U.S. abroad; and
- placed the United States and its allies on the strategic political defensive.

Fighting the war of ideas where the enemy is fighting

Having accepted the enemy's terminology and adopting its definitions as our own, we ceased fighting on our terms and placed our ideas at the enemy's disposal. We are hardly conscious of it. We become defensive and reactive. We pander and sometimes even preemptively capitulate to the whining and carping of certain self-appointed Muslim "leaders" in Western countries, without insisting that they do their part to isolate the extremists in their midst and act as responsible guests and citizens instead of as a special class of victims.

By not understanding the psychopolitical nature of the battle, and by not appreciating the meanings of words, we reward the enemy and demoralize our friends and potential allies. This is very much the case with one of the terms central to today's debate on the war: jihad. These days, most Americans, including national leaders, tend to equate the word with its post-9/11 meaning, that of "holy war," and often use it as a synonym for terrorism. But speakers of Arabic and adherents to Islam are not at all in agreement about this definition. We have an opportunity, then, to "support moderates"(for lack of a better term) by helping re-take the language.

Jihad, in short, may be defined in any number of ways. The terrorist enemy has redefined not only the word, but the idea that it embodies. When U.S. officials use the word, they should be certain about what the enemy takes it to mean, how the non-enemy (i.e., neutral, potential ally or friend) understands its American usage, and how the U.S. wants its target audience and the rest of the world to understand it. By doing so, we can *make jihad work* for the proper ends.

Americans and jihad

Muslim terms are relatively new to the United States. Most Americans first learned of mujahidin, or Islamic holy warriors, with the Soviet takeover of Afghanistan in 1979. They viewed the mujahidin in a positive light, as heroes and brothers-in-arms, in the context of U.S. support and funding for the Muslim fighters battling the Soviet Union.

At roughly the same time, the word jihad entered the daily lexicon, to an entirely different response. *Webster's* existing definition of the time shows how the public understood jihad: as "a holy war waged on behalf of Islam as a religious duty" and "a bitter strife or crusade [sic] undertaken in the spirit of a holy war."[50] Webster's updated the second definition, matter-of-factly and without irony, to mean "a crusade for a principle or belief."[51] Most recently, *Webster's* has preserved the holy war and crusade definitions and added a third: "a personal struggle in devotion to Islam especially involving scriptural discipline."[52]

In truth, the reality is a good deal more complex. Today, the meaning of jihad is so controversial, even or especially within Islam, that interpretations are irreconcilably opposed to one another. Both advocates and critics of terroristic interpretations of jihad can find justification in the Qur'an. Among radical fundamentalists, jihad consists of three levels. One is obligatory warfare to build a global Islamist order (as the Embassy of Saudi Arabia in Washington has

---

[50] *Webster's Third New International Dictionary of the English Language Unabridged* (G&C Merriam Company, 1971).
[51] *Webster's New Collegiate Dictionary* (G & C Merriam Company, 1979).
[52] *Mirriam-Webster Online*, August 2005; *Encyclopedia Britannica* adds, "In the 20th and 21st centuries the concept of jihad has sometimes been used as an ideological weapon in an effort to combat western influences and secular governments and to establish an ideal Islamic society." *Britannica Concise Encyclopedia*, retrieved August 17, 2005 from Encyclopedia Britannica Premium Service.

pronounced in its fundamentalist Wahhabi interpretation).[53] For scriptural fundamentalists, jihad has substantially different meanings, and can refer to childbirth for women and a personal spiritual struggle. More traditionalist Muslims see jihad mainly as a struggle for personal moral improvement, but one that can include warfare on behalf of the faith when "necessary and appropriate." Such a definition is a catch-all, for sure, but one that is open enough for interpretation in advantageous ways.

Reformist traditionalists, for their part, define jihad as a personal, moral journey; only in cases of life or death, or in case of attack or when the survival of Islam is at stake, does jihad become "holy war," according to a dominant view.[54] By contrast, Islamic moderates refer to jihad mainly in terms of personal spiritual development. Secularist Muslims, meanwhile, tend to view jihad as historical phenomena in holy wars of old, and though they accept the term to refer to spiritual improvement they tend to avoid it because of its controversial overtones and underpinnings.[55]

With so many accepted meanings, both within and outside of Islam, the United States has the opportunity to decide how to make the word work for its national interests. Ironically, both Islamist extremists and the United States government currently are content with sharing the narrow, ultra-fundamentalist definition of jihad as terrorism, to the exclusion of the rest of the Islamic world.

But should they be? After all, which idea of jihad does the United States wish to see prevail: the benign and charitable idea of self-improvement and self-discipline, or the idea of total warfare against civilization? The extremists know what they want both Muslims and

---

[53] The Islamic Affairs Department of the Embassy of Saudi Arabia in Washington issued the following exhortation on *jihad* on its website, www.iad.org, in 2003: "Muslims are required to raise the banner of Jihad in order to make the Word of Allah supreme in this world, to remove all forms of injustice and oppression, and to defend the Muslims. If Muslims do not take up the sword, the evil tyrants of this earth will be able to continue oppressing the weak and [the] helpless." The wording no longer appears on the Islamic Affairs Department site, but the Middle East Media Research Institute preserved the statement for the record. See Steven Stalinsky, "The 'Islamic Affairs Department' of the Saudi Embassy in Washington, DC," MEMRI *Special Report* no. 23, November 26, 2003.

[54] Cheryl Benard, *Civil Democratic Islam: Partners, Resources and Strategies* (RAND Corporation, 2003), 12-13.

[55] Ibid.

"the infidel" to believe. Indeed, one can argue that they succeeded long before al Qaeda ever surfaced.

Hijacking jihad

In the late 1970s, Yasser Arafat's Palestine Liberation Organization (PLO) dominated the Middle Eastern terrorist scene. Secular-nationalist in nature, it included non-Muslims (and even an anti-Islam Marxist-Leninist faction). But while members appeared not to mind the killing of those deemed to be collaborators, most Islamic members generally drew the line at the idea of murdering fellow Muslims. Over time, however, new and more extreme groups carried the war beyond Israel to advocate the killing of other Muslims, including women and children, and developed an ideology to justify these tactics in heavily religious terms.

One of the most infamous called itself Islamic Jihad. Founded in Egypt in the late 1970s, Islamic Jihad dedicated itself to the establishment of Islamic rule by force.[56] Its founders chose the group's name purposefully, to convince other Muslims of the legitimacy of their ideology and methods. The name was a conscious effort to justify terrorism in the name of Islam, at a time when most "Muslim terrorists" were terrorists who happened to be Muslim, characterized by the secular PLO, which was mainly motivated by temporal goals of statehood and permanent revolution. Suicide bombing was not a mainstream PLO tactic. Those more extreme than the PLO sought to make their views the norm.

In a manifesto entitled "The Methodology of the Islamic Jihad Group," written in the Turah Penitentiary in Cairo in 1986, Islamic Jihad "group leader" Aboud al-Zumur outlined the organization's semantic strategy.[57] "[W]e chose the term jihad to be part of our name and that people know us by that name, given the fact that 'to struggle' is an essential matter to our movement," Zumur wrote. Basing its ideology on the teachings of 13th century theologian Ibn Taymiyya, the group was careful to establish the religious

---

[56] U.S. Department of State, Office of the Coordinator for Counterterrorism, "Chapter 6 - Terrorist Groups," *Country Reports on Terrorism 2004*, April 27, 2005, www.state.gov/s/ct/rls/45394.htm.
[57] Aboud al-Zumur, *Jama'at al-Jihad al-Islami* (The Methodology of the Islamic Jihad Group) (Cairo, Egypt: Turah Penitentiary, 1986). Translated by the U.S. Department of State.

justifications for its name and actions by getting religious leaders to approve what normal Muslims considered un-Islamic tactics of subversion and violence.

The document explained the Islamic Jihad ideology in careful and legalistic terms, citing archaic theological tracts that repeatedly call for subjecting oneself to "martyrdom," not merely by personal sacrifice but by "giving up one's life." Al-Zumur spelled out the group's beliefs clearly, refuting traditional norms by stressing the un-Islamic methods the group embraced in the quest for political power. He broke some widespread taboos, arguing that Muslim fighters did not need the support of their spiritual leaders, that they could indeed attack non-Muslim civilians, that they could strike offensively and not just in self-defense, and that they could seize political power in foreign countries. In an assault on the sanctity of the family, the Islamic Jihad document said that young Muslims could join the fight against their parents' will and without consent of a duly recognized political authority.

Al-Zumur went even further, arguing that any person or authority who attempts to stop the rogue fighter is himself thwarting the will of God and, by implication, is an infidel who must be killed. The document prepared people that most members of the movement would be expected to die on their mission, either in combat or by suicide, and receive supernatural pleasures in return. Like militant Bolshevism, the "jihad" would be permanent. It would break traditional discipline between young people and their families and spiritual leaders. It would slay Muslim political leaders whom the Islamic Jihad would deem insufficiently Muslim (the group had already assassinated Egyptian President Anwar Sadat). It would install Islamist clerics in their place, justified by the teachings of Shaykh Abu al-Tayyib, a 10th century Muslim poet known for his "panegyrics and masterful manipulation of language."[58]

This new concept of jihad was thus a radical departure from the Muslim status quo and custom. It rejected traditional beliefs about family authority and unity, as well as filial responsibility to parents and siblings, all the while using medieval militant Ibn Tamiyah (considered the inspiration of Wahhabi extremist thought) as its source of moral authority. It demanded a permanent revolution

---

[58] Abu al-Tayyib, 915-965 A.D., is considered among the greatest medieval Arabic poets. The *Bartleby Encyclopedia of World History* recalls al-Tayyib's rousing speeches and manipulation of language.

"until the Day of Judgment" under an elite shock force to overthrow the established political and cultural order. "All Muslim scholars have agreed," the document claimed, that good Muslims should fight and oust present-day governments and "install in their place Muslim spiritual leaders."

Islamic Jihad document shows
Islamist strategy to murder Muslims

The Islamic Jihad's methodology paper indicates the bitter internal battle festering within the Muslim religion. That clash was and is a struggle for legitimacy between the extremism of a fringe group and adherents of traditional Islam. The extremist word games quickly caught on, legitimizing the political goals and creating a new belief system for an emerging generation of the faithful. That new generation would break from their families and the bonds of their established religious leaders to carry out operations, mainly against fellow Muslims, that would result in their own physical destruction.

In calling for the re-definition of jihad, al-Zumur recognized that most Muslims would not accept his extreme interpretations. He called upon his co-religionists to "come to an agreement and understanding about this plan," and urged more senior Muslim figures to join. Those who failed, he admonished, were not following "the messenger of God." The direct implication was that those who disagreed with him were to be treated as apostates who needed to be killed. Those so-called apostates would not die in grace or glory, al-Zumur said; men who failed to join were "remaining in the ranks of women." Muslims who would not be persuaded by reason or faith, he said, must be subjected to ridicule, pain and death.

Innocent people, including and perhaps above all, Muslims, would die, al-Zumur noted. But those very killings were part of the virtue of the new jihad. Under a heading called "Specious Theological Arguments and Their Rebuttal," his document prescribed the circumstances under which a Muslim could legitimately violate traditional moral teachings, including when to lie and cheat, when to associate with those considered the infidel, and even when a good Muslim may kill innocent fellow Muslims. Such killings were virtuous acts, according to the new doctrine, again citing the fountainhead of Wahhabism, because they were creating new martyrs for Allah.

Consequently, such killers in the new Islamic Jihad would go unpunished under Shar'ia law. Indeed, they would be rewarded: "When Muslims fight against non-Muslims, those Muslims who are killed in the battle become martyrs and those who unwittingly kill those who become martyrs do not deserve to be killed. They too become martyrs in the effort to uphold Islam." Muslims who disagree, al-Zumur wrote, "are people who are quite ignorant of their religion."[59]

Bin Laden adopts the new terminology

A decade later, Osama bin Laden would use the same terminology in his 1996 "declaration of war against the United States." The declaration was a political manifesto that demanded the ouster of U.S. forces from Saudi Arabia. "[J]ihad against the infidel in every part of the world, is absolutely essential," he said, to be carried out by "my brothers, the mujahidin, and the sons of the nation."[60] The hijacking of religious terminology, a propaganda victory that silenced more moderate Islamic voices – had the collateral effect of imposing false definitions upon American political discourse regarding the Middle East and the Islamic worlds.

And with predictable results. Without even realizing it, the United States began its post-9/11 counterattack at a political disadvantage, largely because the enemy was first to market in the "war of ideas." In the years since, the United States has only exacerbated this problem. It has undermined civilized Muslims who oppose but fear the extremists by effectively declaring that all practitioners of jihad – and not merely the murderous fringe – were the sworn enemies of the United States. It has validated the enemy's ideological worldview by appearing to declare war on Islam (even as it has taken pains to stress the opposite). And it has given undue power and prestige to the enemy leadership, enhancing their reputations and inspiring more recruits to their cause.

Americans' continuous denunciations of jihad are principled and powerful statements against Islamist terrorism. Such pronouncements are self-affirming and easy to understand.

---

[59] Al-Zumur, op. cit.

[60] Osama bin Laden, "Declaration of War against the Americans Occupying the Land of the Two Holy Places," published in *Al Quds al Arabi* (London), August, 1996.

Americans presume that decent Muslims will readily identify with our mission, but become surprised and angered when they not only fail to support us, but even openly oppose us. By the rules of that rational logic chain, based on a false premise, it is not unreasonable for an unfamiliar person to believe sincerely that most Muslims are terrorists because they either will not fight against jihad or worse, even proclaim their devotion to jihad. Americans' only defense, then, is to declare permanent war on the practitioners of jihad. This is clear and civilized logic to the American. If jihad is aggressive and evil, it must be repulsed.

Washington's defensive offensive

The subject brings us back to Moynihan's concern about semantic infiltration, outlined in the previous chapter, in which we begin to warp our own perceptions by unwittingly adopting the rhetoric of the adversary. Public and official discourse since 9/11 validates the late senator's apprehensions.

In the aftermath of 9/11, the White House properly went to extraordinary lengths to affirm political and diplomatic reality by making clear that the U.S. response to the attacks would not be against "Islam" or against Muslims. However, leaders displayed the inadequacy of their understanding by their occasionally clumsy use of words. Calling for crusade was only a one-time error, quickly corrected. In trying to pre-empt any public manifestations of anti-Muslim sentiment at home while attempting to sound reassuring to the world that the conflict was not a religious one, the administration missed the opportunity to correct the accepted terrorist definition of jihad.[61] All the administration could do was try to calm fears, stoked

---

[61] Meanwhile, the White House public liaison office had a group of self-appointed Muslim "leaders" as a stable for President Bush. None from that group helped correct the administration's mis-portrayal of Muslim terminology, and few if any were active in supporting the war effort. Among the group's leaders was Abdurahman Alamoudi, founder of the American Muslim Council, founder of the Muslim chaplain program in the U.S. military, and financier of several Washington-based Muslim advocacy groups, including the Islamic Free Market Institute founded by a prominent Republican activist. Alamoudi was later convicted in federal court of laundering Libyan money, being part of a terrorist plot to murder the crown prince of Saudi Arabia, and links to other terrorist organizations. The U.S. Department of the Treasury officially linked Alamoudi to al Qaeda in 2005.

by extremist Muslim advocacy groups in many cases,[62] that the U.S. was making war with Islam; it also affirmed that "Islam is a religion of peace" – an assertion that most Americans accustomed to the Islamic Jihad concept were not prepared to believe and which, after being repeated too often, some Muslims found ignorant, patronizing and insincere.

Learning lessons from the post-9/11 rhetoric

A study of statements by the most senior U.S. officials illustrates how the rhetorical, semantic battle was handicapped from the start and offers a lesson on how it might be repaired. Initial statements, especially from the president, were absolutely clear. They established the parameters and nature of the conflict and left no room for misinterpretation. The occasional slip was quickly corrected. But the more the message was refined, the more off-target it became in certain respects. Even after the war effort was well on its way, the semantic blunders continued. Twice in one speech in November, 2003, a senior official made statements containing examples of the influence of semantic infiltration the U.S. leadership's perceptions (emphasis added):

> "Iraq is the central front now in this war on terrorism because with a stable and secure Iraq, *a very hard blow will be dealt to the international jihad*, the international terrorist movement that caused September 11th and intends to continue to pursue us."[63]
> We have a very good strategy for dealing with this upsurge of violence in Iraq. We know that we're dealing with regime remnants.

---

[62] Western Muslim groups did themselves no favors in responding to the 9/11 attacks. Top U.S. Muslim organizations in Washington made public demands that the FBI and other authorities defend them from an expected rash of hate crimes (which never happened) instead of offering all their collective talents and knowledge to help U.S. security and intelligence services to hunt down the perpetrators. They did not offer to help officially until three weeks after the attacks, when the FBI sent out a call for people with native fluency to serve as paid translators. Thus the groups set their communities apart from the rest of the country from the very beginning and cast suspicion on themselves and on Muslims and Arab-Americans in general, while complaining loudly about such suspicions. There were exceptions to this rule, but they were few.

[63] The White House, "Interview of the National Security Advisor by KHOU-TV, Houston, Texas," 10 November 2003. Emphasis added.

We're dealing with some foreign terrorists, who are coming in from outside the country to fight what they believe is an extremely important jihad.[64]

In 2004 through the third anniversary of the 9/11 attacks, top U.S. officials repeated the jihad rhetoric. The statements appear designed to educate domestic audiences about the nature of the threat:

"With respect to the al Qaeda organization, or to a *terrorist who is committed to jihad, who is out to kill infidels* and is prepared to sacrifice their life in the process, the whole notion of deterrence is meaningless."[65]

"They are *absolutely committed to jihad, to killing infidels.* We're at the top of the list."[66]

"A handful of the people, *motivated by an intense desire to commit jihad, to kill the infidel* - and we're the infidel."[67]

"These are people who are *absolutely committed to jihad and that want to kill infidels* and we're the infidels."[68]

"As I say, it's a tough, long, hard slog. . . . There's nothing you can hold at risk that will deter them from attacking us. *They're committed to jihad. They want to kill infidels. That's us. . . .*"[69]

The vice president, who made the above statements, clearly and carefully showed that the war is with extremists who are themselves making war on traditional Islam. Again, the message might have been lost on Muslim audiences, even though the speaker was precise in all but the last sentence:

---

[64] The White House, "Interview of the National Security Advisor by KXAS-TV, Dallas, Texas," 10 November 2003. Emphasis added.

[65] The White House, 14 September 2004. "Vice President's Remarks and Q&A at a Town Hall Meeting in Ottumwa, Iowa." Emphasis added.

[66] The White House, 17 September 2004. Emphasis added.

[67] The White House, "Vice President and Mrs. Cheney's Q & A in Johnstown, Pennsylvania," 18 October 2004. Emphasis added.

[68] The White House, "Vice President and Mrs. Cheney's Q & A in Cincinnati, Ohio," 19 October 2004. Emphasis added.

[69] The White House, "Vice President and Mrs. Cheney Q & A in Cedar Rapids, Iowa," 23 October 2004. Emphasis added.

This is a global conflict that is being perpetrated by a radical fringe that's got an extremist ideology based on the far-out fringes of the Islamic faith, not at all representative of Islam. But – and they are prepared to kill anybody who stands in their way, and they've done it. And they will continue to do it. It isn't a group you can negotiate with. There's no treaty at the end of the day. There aren't going to be any Paris Peace Accords that are going to put an end to this. These are non-state actors. There's not a government to negotiate with here. *These are people who are absolutely committed to jihad and that want to kill infidels and we're the infidels.*[70]

The administration wasn't alone in speaking in such terms. Political leaders from both parties, officials in law enforcement, intelligence, diplomacy and the armed forces, and major news organizations all used similar rhetoric. Significantly, the groups purporting to represent Muslims nationwide, whom the White House and the opposition party had tapped for counsel on Islamic affairs, made no visible attempt to disabuse officials and the media about the choices of words. Some smaller groups, as well as individuals, did, but were not heeded.

Toward a new vocabulary

If not jihad, then what? If foreign terrorists are not, in truth, holy warriors but rather mass murderers, what do we call them, and what should our message to the rest of the Muslim world be?

Tilting the playing field requires undermining the enemy and destroying its ideas – not merely refuting them or "competing" with them in an intellectual "marketplace." So far, the United States has fallen far short of this objective, contenting itself with trying to convince Muslims throughout the Islamic world of its good intentions. Such an approach is profoundly self-defeating. The objective should not be to try and convince skeptical Muslims that the U.S. is not engaged in a "war against Islam," but to show, relentlessly and in the most vivid terms, that the extremists are un-

---

[70] The White House, "Vice President and Mrs. Cheney's Remarks and Q&A at a Roundtable Discussion in Cincinnati, Ohio," 19 October 2004. Emphasis added.

Islamic and that the nations of the great Abrahamic religions are united against a common mortal enemy.

By necessity, the American political counterattack in the "war of ideas" should be geared toward depriving radical elements of their ability to dominate religious semantics and rhetoric. In so doing, the U.S. will be helping to destroy the image of the enemy as hero – a crucial mechanism currently fueling the fight against the United States and its Coalition partners.

Doing so means adjusting U.S. rhetoric so as not to hinder civilized Muslims in the recovery of their ideas. If the current idea of jihad as terrorism is offensive to the average Muslim, who sees the same word as a just and good action blessed by God, then the U.S. must find another word to describe its enemy and its actions.

Not as religious terms, but as political

James Guirard, a Washington-based political operative and wordsmith, has spent years consulting with Muslim clerics, Arabic scholars and others to develop a new vocabulary that, if used boldly and consistently, could shift the terms of debate in the Arabic-speaking and Islamic worlds and marginalize the terrorists from their support networks. The vocabulary could diminish the radicals' stature and appeal to young prospective recruits. And use of it could sow uncertainty among the recruits about one another, their leaders, and their cause.

Such an approach would help our allies and would-be allies in the Arab and Muslim worlds. Though senior State Department officials with direct responsibility for message-making have been dismissive of the ideas to take back the language, citing their own anonymous Arabic consultants, many Muslims and scholars of Islam agree strongly with the ideas behind Guirard's persistent approach. Carnegie scholar Asma Afsaruddin, Associate Professor of Arabic and Islamic Studies at the University of Notre Dame, has been studying the semantic content of jihad. She observes:

> The important battle of semantics is not about window-dressing but about reclaiming the true meaning of jihad – which refers to the noblest human 'struggle' or 'endeavor' to realize God's will for a just and merciful society on earth – from those who would willfully abuse it. The Qur'anic and classical notion of jihad signifies a continuing enterprise on the part of the religious to uphold what was good and resist what is evil: this enterprise, is,

after all, at the root of every civilized society and thus ultimately conducive to true peace.[71]

Hirabah: The un-jihad

The United States, then, must find ideas already in the Arabic language and Muslim culture that can be applied to describe Islamist terror. Fortunately, a thousand years of Islamic jurisprudence has already provided us with the proper word: *hirabah*. As Layla Sein of the Association of Muslim Social Scientists explains:

> Since the concept of jihad comes from the root word *jahada* (to strive or struggle for self-betterment from an ethical-moral perspective) and that of hirabah comes from the root word *hariba* (to fight, to go to war or become enraged or angry), an etymological and theological examination of these words provides a valid framework through which the religious legitimacy of suicide bombings in today's global community can be analyzed...

> To delve into a comparative study of these Islamic concepts is to expose how hirabah is being paraded by terrorist groups as jihad. By defining hirabah as jihad, such terrorist groups as al Qaeda and others promote their terrorist agendas by misleading young, religiously motivated and impressionable Muslims to believe that killing unarmed and non-combatant civilians are activities of jihad, and hence a ticket to paradise...

> If activities of fear and terror associated with hirabah are used to define the meaning of jihad in hopes of recruiting Muslim youth to undertake suicide bombings and other criminal activities, Muslim theologians need to define the nature of what is happening to stop the hijacking of Islam by terrorists.[72]

"Given the all too common tendency to employ jihad and terrorism as synonymous," says Antony T. Sullivan, of the Center for Middle Eastern and North African Studies at the University of

---

[71] Asma Afsaruddin, letter to Jim Guirard. The author acknowledges Guirard for providing many of the quotations used in this chapter. Guirard's website is www.truespeak.org.

[72] Layla Sein, "Editorial," Association of Muslim Social Scientists *AMSS Bulletin* 3, no. 4 (2002).

Michigan, "there is now perhaps no traditional Islamic concept that cries out louder for revival than hirabah."[73]

Hirabah would be more appropriate and useful, not only for public diplomacy or political reasons, but for the purpose of destroying terrorist networks. U.S. federal law enforcement officials refer to Islamist terrorists as "jihadis," as do the Armed Forces and counterterrorism strategists. This, University of Michigan Professor Abdul Hakim argued immediately after 9/11 in an important article on classical Islamic law on terrorism, is a misnomer:

> hirabah appears... to parallel the function of terrorism as an American legal category... hirabah actually goes beyond the FBI definition of terrorism, inasmuch as hirabah covers both directed and coincidental spreading of fear... Hirabah, as it turns out, is the most severely punished crime in Islam, carrying mandatory criminal sanctions.[74]

So using the proper Arabic term could help legitimize extreme measures to take down the terrorists. Hakim writes that "the severest punishments . . . are explicitly outlined in Qur'an 5:33-34, virtually the beginning and end of all juristic discussions on hirabah." The punishments include execution, crucifixion, or amputation of hands and feet, the latter for humiliation in this life and for "grievous chastisement" in the next.[75]

One finds little doubt, then, that many Muslims are comfortable with the idea of hirabah as a proper means of demonizing those we call "jihadis." Immediately after the September 11th attacks, Dr. Ezzeddin Ibrahim, the former chancellor of Al Ain University in Abu Dhabi, United Arab Emirates, made the point that:

> What occurred on September 11, 2001, is one of the most loathsome of crimes, which in Islam goes under the name of al-hirabah. Hirabah is the most abominable type of murder, in that it involves killing with terrorism and intimidation.[76]

---

[73] Antony T. Sullivan, letter to Jim Guirard.

[74] Sherman A. Jackson (a.k.a. Abdul Hakim), "Domestic Terrorism in the Islamic Legal Tradition," *Muslim World*, Vol. 91, No. 3/4, Fall 2001, pp. 293-310.

[75] Ibid.

[76] "Excerpt: Interview with Ezzeddin Ibrahim," *Middle East Policy Council Journal*, Vol. VIII, No. 4, December 2001.

Guirard collected and solicited quotes on hirabah from scholars of Islam and Arab culture around the world to indicate the scope of resonance. While some of the quotes show differences of opinion on the precise meaning of jihad, they are unanimous that jihad does not mean what the extremists (and the U.S. government) say it means, and that hirabah is the appropriate term. Professor Akbar Ahmed, Chair of Islamic Studies at the American University, concurs:

> Properly understood, this is a war of ideas within Islam – some of them faithful to authentic Islam, but some of them clearly un-Islamic and even blasphemous toward the peaceful and compassionate Allah of the Qur'an... As a matter of truth-in-Islam, both the ideas and the actions they produce must be called what they actually are, beginning with the fact that al Qaeda's brand of suicide mass murder and its fomenting of hatred among races, religions and cultures do not constitute godly or holy 'jihad' – but, in fact, constitute the heinous crime and sin of unholy 'hirabah'... such ungodly 'war against society' should be condemned as blasphemous and un-Islamic.[77]

Even some Saudi-associated Muslim organizations are in agreement about the use of the word (though some Saudi-funded scholars and organizations in the U.S. are not). One such group is the Islamic Society of North America (ISNA), one of the most influential Muslim groups in the United States and Canada – and reportedly an important promoter of more fundamentalist, even extremist, forms of Islam, with extensive Saudi Arabian funding.[78] According to ISNA Secretary General Sayyid M. Syeed:

> The Qur'an and the sayings of the prophet emphatically distinguished the term jihad from hirabah, a destructive act of rebellion committed against God and mankind. Hirabah is an act of terrorism, a subversive act inflicted by an individual or a gang of individuals, breaking the established norms of peace, civic laws, treaties, agreements, moral and ethical codes... While as

---

[77] Akbar Ahmed, letter to Jim Guirard.

[78] Matthew Levitt, "Subversion from Within: Saudi Funding of Islamic Extremist Groups Undermining U.S. Interests and the War on Terror from Within the United States," Testimony before the Subcommittee on Terrorism, Technology and Homeland Security of the Committee on the Judiciary, United States Senate, September 10, 2003.

different forms of jihad are highly commendable acts of virtue, hirabah is respected as a despicable crime... *Individuals and groups indulging in hirabah are condemned as criminals, subjected to severe deterrent punishments under Islamic law and warned of far more punishment and humiliation in the life after life.*[79] (Emphasis added)

Syeed's statement is especially important. His organization is the largest supplier of Saudi-funded Islamic literature in more than 1,100 North American mosques, and the source of much of the ideologically extreme interpretations of Islam to include the Salafist/Wahhabi interpretations of jihad. Whether ISNA is trying to debunk the radical interpretation of policy is another matter.

"Think of the disincentive to young, hungry, cynical Muslims – angry at their own governments and angry at ours for bolstering theirs," notes Anisa Mehdi, a journalist who produced the documentary "Inside Mecca" for National Geographic Television. "If they heard 'hirabah' instead of 'jihad,' if they heard 'murder' instead of 'martyr,' if they heard they were bound for hell not heaven, they might not be so quick to sign up to kill themselves and a handful of so-called 'infidels' along the way."[80]

A quick and no-cost offensive

It takes little effort and no money to change the rhetoric and the thinking about jihad, hirabah, and related Islamic terminology that shape and define ideas. There need be no bureaucratic restructuring, no congressional appropriations or approval, no turf battles; just awareness from public officials and a substitution of words.

To that end, the president and other senior officials can and should take the lead in changing the rhetoric of the "War on Terror." Their statements will generate headlines, controversy, and ultimately reflection around the world. Even without purporting to be authorities on the language or ideology, they will promote, without directly intervening in, the raging debate within Islam. U.S. leaders should also help to properly define jihad and hirabah in U.S.

---

[79] Sayyid M. Syeed, letter to Jim Guirard, cited by Guirard, "Properly Condemning the al Qaeda Blasphemy," *The American Muslim*, April 21, 2003.
[80] Anisa Mehdi, "Let's Rescue a Once-Beautiful Word from Its Captors," *Star-Ledger* (Newark), December 29, 2004.

government glossaries and directories, and enforce the rhetorical change throughout the United States government, including the Departments of Defense, State and Justice, as well as the counterterrorism and law-enforcement agencies within them.

Elected officials should also promote a similar transformation abroad. In particular, they should constantly press the Saudi government, and Saudi-funded entities like ISNA, to renounce the pro-terrorist interpretations of jihad, revive the concept of hirabah, and then identify and marginalize practitioners of hirabah and those who support them. The U.S. is entitled to make this challenge because Saudi state propaganda has fueled the justification of terrorism in the name of jihad around the world, and especially in and against the United States. Simultaneously, Washington should make a point of highlighting the works of journalists, commentators, clerics and others around the world that denounce Islamist terrorism as hirabah – and promote similar steps among Muslims at large.

Timing and expansion of vocabulary

The timing, as of this writing, is just right for the new semantic offensive. The "insurgents" in Iraq have so clearly waged hirabah against Iraqi society, with the vast majority of their intended victims being not Americans but Muslim Iraqi Arabs, including children, that Muslims around the world are recognizing the nature of the enemy. Arab satellite television coverage, including on Aljazeera and Saudi-run al Arabiya, had stopped, if briefly, promoting the "insurgents" by mid-2005 and showed them as murderers of innocent people.

Again, good message-making could lead to a tipping point: that coverage has yet to show the Americans sympathetically, although al Arabiya on occasion has positively portrayed British troops in Iraq.[81] And Aljazeera has been going out of its way to feature many different points of view as it tries to become more accepted as a legitimate media organization.

Meanwhile, the suicide bombings of the Madrid subway in 2004, the London transit system in July 2005, and attacks in Egypt, Indonesia, Turkey, Bangladesh, Jordan, Iraq and elsewhere finally provoked visible, organized, and sustained expressions of outrage

---

[81] Sebastian Usher, "Iraq Violence Shifting Arab Media Coverage," BBC, June 23, 2005.

and rejection among previously silent Muslim leaders worldwide. American public diplomacy and strategic communication should amplify the messages relentlessly through every rational venue, and help form a climate by which such denunciations become the norm, and where the silent must decide whether to speak up or remain on the fringes.

Once the proper ideas of jihad and hirabah are more widely known and accepted, the rest flows logically and easily. One by one we take the key words that define the core ideas of the enemy's belief system and use them to discredit the terrorists and, more importantly, the terrorist ideology that provides not only the psychological support system for the bombers, but the intellectual and emotional base that nurtures and reinforces the terrorists' hostile will.

If people accept that the terrorists are not fighting a just and holy war but rather are waging a campaign of murder against humanity, then the terrorists are not *mujahidin* holy warriors. If they are not mujahidin, they will not die as martyrs (*shahiddin*). If they are neither holy nor martyrs, they bring their families not glory but disgrace. They bring the Muslim people not respect but hardship. They portray Mohammed's teachings to be not of charity and mercy but of absolute evil, and in so doing, they wish not peace upon the prophet but disgrace. They do not glorify Allah, but defile him. And they might even prove that the Americans are right.

Mufsidoon, tajdeef, Shaitaniyya

So if the terrorists really are not shahiddin and mujahidin, then what should we call them? Again, as Guirard points out, the Qur'an provides the word: *mufsidoon* (moof-see-DOON), or condemned evildoers.[82] And mufsidoon who distort the Qur'an for their own twisted ends are not faithful servants of God but blasphemers committing *tajdeef*, members of a cult waging hirabah. Mufsidoon serve not Allah but Satan (*shaitan*). Sullivan adds:

---

[82] President George W. Bush used the word "evildoers" in early post-9/11 rhetoric, but the State Department made no attempt to popularize the word in Arabic (mufsidoon) or any other language, and the concept all but disappeared form senior officials' vocabulary, including that of the president.

Tajdeef designates the blasphemy that results from the waging of unholy warfare by evildoers. Tajdeef has traditionally been considered by Muslims as an act of apostasy punishable by death. . . . Tajdeef and the activities of mufsidoon have been understood by Muslims as examples of *Shaitaniyya*, or Satanic and anti-Islamic activity.[83]

Therefore, not only does Islam permit the just execution or combat killing of mufsidoon – thus legitimizing or at least mitigating the lethal side of U.S. and allied counterterrorism policy – but once the mufsidoon are dead, their souls go not to blissful paradise with 72 beautiful virgins, but to an eternity of pain and humiliation in the eternal hellfire of *Jahannam*.

Islamic admonitions to religious young men, Guirard argues, should be: *Do not wage hirabah, do not become mufsidoon, do not commit tajdeef, do nothing that would cause Allah to cast you into Jahannam*. The U.S. government lacks the proper standing to issue religious interpretations of any nature. Such official statements are not only bad policy but, as military public affairs officers constantly if spuriously admonish, may raise constitutional issues.

And then the Arabic language and its poetic traditions offer endless word plays that might make no sense to the non-speaker, but that resonate in their cultural home. An example recognizable to the English ear would be to take "Wahhabi" and pair it poetically with *irhabi*, which means "terrorist."

For U.S. government purposes, the theology supplies only an understanding of the logic chain. In practical terms, the vernacular is a political device in the ideological conflict. When the proper debate begins, American image-makers can pick up on the terminology, using the words casually in their commentary. The U.S. then reports on those debates to foreign audiences in its public diplomacy, international broadcasting, information operations and other channels. It should report on those words confidently and relentlessly, taking care to amplify enough different voices (and encourage more) so that individuals do not either personalize the issue or become targets for ostracism or worse. The U.S. can give ample airtime, translated in dozens of languages, over its vast global

---

[83] Sullivan, p. 19.

television, radio and Internet networks, including English. Strong precedent exists for such practices.[84]

Muslims are already acting in a more public and coordinated manner to combat the extremists. Under the sponsorship of King Abdullah of Jordan, 170 Muslim scholars from 40 countries met in July, 2005, in an attempt to unify the schools of Islamic thought and to prevent clerics of one sect from denouncing others as *takfeer* or apostates. The takfeer denunciations have been popular instrument of the terrorists and their spiritual leaders to justify their extremism and violence. The participants issued a statement in which they "tried to limit the religious approach used by militants to justify their violence through regulating the interpretation of Islam and issuing religious edicts."[85] Here, U.S. public diplomacy did amplify the messages from the conference.

Other Muslim figures have begun taking a contrary approach. They have mustered the courage to identify extremists by name and denounce them as apostates, issuing fatwas in the harshest of terms and "excommunicating" the extremists, so to speak, as being no longer Muslim. This is an important development that we will discuss in Chapter 6. The bottom line is that the debates within Islam have geopolitical implications. The U.S. is therefore entitled and obligated to encourage, amplify and protect the voices against the extremists. American officials and opinion-makers themselves must use the vocabulary in the correct English and non-English contexts for the reinforcement and acceleration of these messages.

---

[84] The U.S. established precedents for quoting religious leaders' theological statements that comported with government policy throughout the Cold War, as part of public diplomacy and political warfare to defeat extremism. Those precedents include the broadcasting of religious services to targeted populations around the world. The U.S. government actively supported the Catholic political party in Italy, the Christian Democrats, in the 1948 election to defeat the Communists. In the 1980s the U.S. reached out to Catholic and Protestant clergy to inform and encourage debate on the need to modernize the nuclear deterrence against the Soviet Union. Another measure supported the Polish Catholic underground, in quiet cooperation with the Vatican. The U.S. government injected itself into an intra-Christian, and even intra-Catholic politico-theological debate, "liberation theology" of the 1980s that legitimized and encouraged Marxist-Leninist revolutionary movements in developing countries.

[85] Sana Abdallah, "Muslim scholars 'forbid' labeling apostasy," United Press International, July 6, 2005.

We can make jihad an ally against terrorism. The enemy has succeeded in changing key definitions in language, and consequently in changing entire people's perceptions of ideas, by warping the language of the Qur'an and of historical Islam. Americans have adopted the extremists' definition of key words, and therefore of the terrorists' ideas. However, the linguistic and cultural foundations of the societies in which the terrorists flourish offer powerful weapons *against* the enemy.

Conclusion

Islamic words, ideas, laws and customs can be the United States' best ally in the war as long as they are properly understood, used in the proper cultural context, deployed by spokespersons with message authority, and relentlessly magnified and repeated. Mastery of the proper vocabulary is vital in U.S. message-making for several reasons. The proper vocabulary:

- will help break the extremists' domination of the idea of jihad and martyrdom, the very ideas that bolster the will to murder;
- will help restore a non-violent way for people to manifest their fears and anxieties, hopes and aspirations;
- will sow doubt and division in the extremists' support bases, and increase collaboration with international counterterrorism authorities;[86]
- may cause some extremists before, during and after recruitment to begin questioning their ideology and the consequences of their "martyrdom";
- will strengthen the traditional scholars and clergy, and the politicians and peoples who follow them;
- will help offer a Qur'anic justification for uniting in a war against the terrorists;
- will help break the spirit and will of the enemy; and
- will help to discredit and ultimately destroy the viability of the enemy's ideology and ideas.

Inaccurate or inappropriate use of language, or unwillingness to make full and proper use of languages and terms as rhetorical

---

[86] Such divisions provide important opportunities for intelligence collection and must be exploited for collection and operational purposes.

devices and weapons in their own right, serves the enemy. Re-capturing and preserving the proper meanings of words can discredit and negate the power of the enemy's ideas, especially among the populations where the enemy recruits and operates. At the same time, the proper use of words provides positive, unifying themes that cater to local cultures and strengthen civil societies. Words can be the ultimate precision guided weapons in the war of ideas: they can be deployed to the targets immediately, require no bureaucratic reorganization, and cost nothing. The barriers to their proper use include ignorance, political correctness and the unwillingness of officials to make words work to help win the war.

4

Branding the enemy

Introduction

Branding – the art of conditioning an audience to associate a given product, person or idea with a desired cognitive or emotional response – can be an important part of developing messages. The State Department public diplomacy shop attempted to "brand" the U.S. after 9/11, but after negligible and arguably counterproductive results, it quietly abandoned the effort.

The branding idea, however, is sound. In the commercial marketplace of ideas, branding is a proven path to success, and the failure to brand can put one out of business. Failure to brand also runs the risk that our enemies will successfully brand us themselves in ways that reinforce the myths, misperceptions and deceits that they already deploy against us. It is time to try branding again. This time, though, the U.S. should start with a message that its audiences are most likely to accept readily: the evil nature of the enemy. Reinforcement of that negative "brand" can put the competitor out of business, and sets the stage for greater audience receptivity to positive follow-on messages about the United States itself.

We will look at the following points in this chapter:

- Effective branding of an enemy will diminish his image among his followers and the concentric rings of support and sympathy, and ultimately aid in the enemy's physical defeat.
- Such branding will be aimed at followers of extremists in the proper cultural contexts.
- Rallying of domestic support against the enemy must be done in a way that does not undermine branding abroad aimed at the target's support base.

- Constant, personal attacks on the enemy by the improper authorities can aid the enemy by building his brand;
- Successive presidents of a superpower branded the enemy in ways that strengthened the enemy's brand and eroded the image of the office of the presidency;
- The war effort itself must be branded so as to maximize domestic and international support, and minimize the potential for organized opposition at home and abroad;
- Part of the branding effort involves recapturing the language in the contested battlespaces; and
- Government policies must be crafted in ways that do not contradict or inflict damage on the credibility of the war effort brand.

In some types of commercial and political branding, an effective approach is not to collect endorsements but denunciations. Vilification from one's opponents can be just as valuable, if not more valuable, as praise from a supporter. In these types of campaigns the negative is a strong, emotional, energizing, and unifying factor in building support where a positive message is insufficient. Indeed, our enemies have used our ineffective denunciations to inflict further damage on our image and reinforce and magnify their message.

In American politics, each side can benefit from denouncing the other, and each side can gain from the other's denunciations. Campaign veterans say that the systematic telling of unpleasant truths about the opponent, what some call negative campaigning, can be crucial: If you can't win, at least you can make your opponent lose. Nevertheless, American candidates and the electorate generally prefer more positive and genteel messages. Here is where third-party voices again become important, where others can create and sustain powerful negative messages against the opponent while keeping the candidate and his persona (or in the war effort, the United States or the president and top leaders) above the unseemliness of it all.

Branding the enemy

The first rule in branding the enemy, as with all message-making, must be to avoid inflicting harm upon oneself. The United States has declared that terrorism, terror, or extremism, regardless of ideology, are the enemies of mankind. Official policy is to lead a war of the world's civilized people against those who use extremism and terrorism as a means of influencing events or seeking power. While much disagreement remains over the scope and definitions, the overall U.S. message has been firm and clear, making the Afghanistan campaign and international counterterrorism cooperation relatively uncontroversial considering the breadth of the coalition.[87]

Equally clear is the American "branding" of more specific terrorist enemies. President Bill Clinton in the mid-1990s first named Osama bin Laden and the al Qaeda organization as great dangers to the United States. In doing so, the president helped draw an obscure businessman-turned-terrorist from the relative anonymity of his network in Sudan and Afghanistan to become one of the most ubiquitous names and faces on Earth.

Bin Laden was one of countless extremists seeking to lead a global "jihad" against the United States and its allies, but he offered both material resources and a greater vision beyond a holy land or geographic area to impose his particular view of Islam on the rest of the world. He also had a track record and a following. He practiced what he preached. His interest went far beyond the Israel-Palestine conflict. His ideology therefore held a global appeal to those contemplating revisionist "jihad." He threatened not merely (or even principally) the "Zionists" and their allies but all those whom he deemed insufficiently Muslim.

With minimal investment in the propaganda machinery that most political groups and leaders must build to attract and maintain recognition, bin Laden and his associates let their actions speak for

---

[87] Much of the domestic and international consensus supporting the U.S. in the "Global War on Terrorism" quickly broke down over Iraq. The U.S. administration clearly stated from the outset that it was making war against practitioners and state sponsors of terrorism in general, and not simply against those responsible for the September 11, 2001 attacks; its near-exclusive focus on al Qaeda and allied Islamists (at the expense, for example, of non-Islamist terrorists like the FARC in Colombia) nevertheless gave the impression that "terrorism" meant bin Laden and his allies. While the U.S. administration portrayed Iraq as part of the global terrorism problem and, indeed, maintained the Saddam Hussein regime on the State Department list of state sponsors of terror, its narrow and legalistic focus on weapons of mass destruction and violations of United Nations resolutions led to public perceptions that Iraq was a separate issue from terrorism.

themselves. They built a global following through personal networking, published tracts and websites in the ummah, seldom if ever issuing any statements in English and relying on others, both friend and foe, to create and market their "brand."

Their most powerful propaganda was that, unlike other Arab or Muslim leaders, they actually brought the fight directly to their perceived oppressors. Bin Laden's August 1996 *fatwa* declaring war, though titled as a war against U.S. "occupiers" in Saudi Arabia, site of the two holy cities of Mecca and Medina, declared war on the world. In addition to attacking the United States, al Qaeda's declaration spanned from Europe, across Africa, the Middle East and Eurasia, to Southeast Asia, warring against Muslim and non-Muslim alike. Bin Laden proclaimed:

> It should not be hidden from you that the people of Islam had suffered from aggression, iniquity and injustice imposed on them by the Zionist-Crusaders alliance and their collaborators; to the extent that the Muslims' blood became the cheapest and their wealth as loot in the hands of the enemies. Their blood was spilled in Palestine and Iraq. The horrifying pictures of the massacre of Qana, in Lebanon are still fresh in our memory. Massacres in Tajikistan, Burma, Kashmir, Assam, the Philippines, Fatani, Ogaden, Somalia, Eritrea, Chechnya and in Bosnia-Herzegovina took place, massacres that send shivers in the body and shake the conscience. All of this and the world watch and hear, and not only didn't respond to these atrocities, but also with a clear conspiracy between the USA and its allies and under the cover of the iniquitous United Nations, the dispossessed people were even prevented from obtaining arms to defend themselves.

> The people of Islam awakened and realized that they are the main target for the aggression of the Zionist-Crusaders alliance. All false claims and propaganda about 'Human Rights' were hammered down and exposed by the massacres that took place against the Muslims in every part of the world. . . .

> . . . I say to the [U.S.] Secretary of Defense [William Cohen]: The sons of the land of the two Holy Places [Mecca and Medina] had come out to fight against the Russian in Afghanistan, the Serb in Bosnia-Herzegovina, and today they are fighting in Chechnya and – by the permission of Allah – they have been made victorious

over your partner, the Russians. By the command of Allah, they
are also fighting in Tajikistan.[88]

Thus before his big 1998 debut as the mastermind of the bombings
of the American embassies in Kenya and Tanzania, bin Laden
created the political context of himself as an uncompromising
defender of all Muslims everywhere.

He gave no credit to the non-Muslim and predominantly Christian
countries that helped fight the Soviets in Afghanistan, or battled and
stabilized the former Yugoslavia on behalf of the Bosnian Muslims
and the Kosovars. He drew no distinction between predominantly
Christian countries that sided with Muslims in conflicts against
nominally Christian armies led by atheist rulers. He publicly
cautioned against Muslim-on-Muslim violence even as he justified
the same in the name of wiping out collaborators with the infidel.[89]
For his target audience in the worldwide ummah, some would
perceive his message as positive and inspirational, even uplifting.

Bin Laden branded himself as a liberator against the Americans
who propped up the corrupt regime in Saudi Arabia first, and
secondarily the Zionists in Israel. The declaration was an ambitious
political agenda for the black sheep of a prominent Saudi family, a
man without a country hiding in Sudan and Afghanistan, a sociopath
on the fringes of the fringe. Indeed bin Laden had a substantial
following of tens of thousands who went through his terrorism and
ideological training camps, but to most Muslims he was a dangerous
threat.

The American message played into bin Laden's hands. President
Bill Clinton's rhetoric elevated the terrorist from obscurity and
disgrace to rhetorical peer status with the leader of the world's sole
superpower. White House rhetoric from Clinton and Bush degraded
the status of the president to bin Laden's level. It poured the
foundation of the U.S. message, and cemented the davidian stature
of bin Laden, that both sides built upon ever since.

---

[88] Osama bin Laden, "Declaration of War against the Americans Occupying
the Land of the Two Holy Places," fatwa published in *Al Quds Al Arabi*
(London), August, 1996, trans.
[89] Ibid. In his fatwa, bin Laden identifies the Saudi "regime" and its
security forces, among others, as targets for attack.

Branding terrorist leaders

The U.S. lacked or failed to deploy the intelligence and military capabilities to kill or capture bin Laden and destroy al Qaeda after the 1993 World Trade Center bombing and 1998 embassy bombings in Africa, or the 2000 bombing of the *USS Cole* in Yemen. It chose not to accept Sudan's offer to hand over the terrorist, citing the Khartoum regime's own record. As a stopgap, the U.S. might have tried to diminish bin Laden's prestige. Instead, it did the opposite, branding him Public Enemy Number One. Osama bin Laden's name and face became world-famous not simply on the FBI's Most Wanted list or a low-level State Department report, but through repeated personal pronouncements of the President of the United States and his senior cabinet members. The half-hearted and useless U.S. military responses, usually cruise missile attacks on soft targets like a Sudanese factory and empty training camps, showed weakness and inflated the terrorist's stature further.

Not since Fidel Castro took power nearly half a century before had so insignificant an entity become the focus such a personal and sustained verbal attack of an American president. Presidential rhetoric helped bin Laden convert himself in much of the ummah and beyond from a wayward son or common nuisance to an underdog of sorts.[90] The American branding intensified after every

---

[90] President Reagan's brush-off of Libyan dictator Muammar Qaddafi as a "flaky barbarian" is an example of presidential rhetoric to diminish the standing of a terrorist leader, and as a chief of state, Qaddafi was already a diplomatic peer of the president. Reagan did not personally denounce figures from terrorist organizations as two of his successors have done. The author argues that *any* presidential identification of a terrorist by name serves only to elevate the extremist and diminish the presidency. A good example of proper presidential political treatment of extremists is the Bush Administration's public policy toward Venezuelan dictator Hugo Chavez. Although Chavez has tried ambitiously to provoke the U.S., the Bush Administration has been careful not to make any personal reference to him, even after the 2006 United Nations speech. The policy allowed others to take Chavez down a peg (such as a surprise rebuke from Harlem Congressman Charles Rangel) and in Latin America, where the U.S. denied the Venezuelan the opportunity to cloak himself as an underdog being picked on by Yankee imperialism. This policy stands in vivid contrast to the highly personalized presidential and cabinet-level attacks on individual al Qaeda leaders.

al Qaeda attack, from the embassies in East Africa and the *Cole*, and again under a second American president from the other political party after 9/11.

The inadvertent presidential elevation of bin Laden from nobody to überterrorist set the stage for unintentionally raising the prestige of other extremists. Having adopted some of the terrorists' distorted jargon as the official American definition, senior U.S. figures would soon "brand" other terrorists by name, elevating them, too, as in this instance in early 2004:

> Because people like [Abu Musab-al] Zarqawi and their al Qaeda affiliates and their al Qaeda colleagues know that when Iraq is stable and peaceful and prosperous and democratic, that we will blow a huge hole in their sense of inevitability for this murderous jihad that they're trying to carry out. That's why Zarqawi and those people are in and if you think for one minute that if we weren't in Iraq, they were just going to be someplace drinking tea? No. (Laughter.) They were going to be fighting the jihad somewhere.[91]

Yet at the same time on the re-election campaign trail, President Bush went out of his way not to name his "opponent," Senator John Kerry. White House and campaign strategists reasoned that identifying Kerry by name would be beneath the office of the presidency, would lower Bush's own personal status versus his challenger, and would help elevate Kerry's status and his campaign. The president relied on surrogates to make the personal attacks. This was a sound message strategy in a very close campaign.

And just as a good political campaign has an effective opposition research operation to discredit the rival, the U.S. government has a fine opposition research team ready to deploy against the enemy. However, the federal government not made optimal use of information already at its fingertips. In one of many examples of where tunnel vision damaged the war effort, U.S. intelligence compiled an excellent 200-page collection of Osama bin Laden's statements, yet the government never released the compilation to the public due to copyright concerns.[92] A simplified collection of bin

---

[91] The White House, "Remarks by National Security Advisor Dr. Condoleezza Rice to the Reagan Lecture," 26 February 2004.

[92] The document is titled "Compilation of Usama bin Ladin Statements, 1994-January 2004," produced by the Foreign Broadcast Information Service (FBIS) and published in January, 2004. It is marked "For Official

Laden quotes shows a decade-long pattern of a man who uses Islam for political purposes while being an apostate or unbeliever (*kafir*). Apparently, no one thought to secure copyright permissions from the quoted news organizations the way normal publishers do, or requested that a lawmaker insert the quotes in the *Congressional Record* or in the proceedings of a hearing that would moot the copyright issue.

Bin Laden appears more worried about losing his prestige among Muslims than he is about losing his life to the Americans. On several occasions he has made statements defending himself against allegations of apostasy and blasphemy. If this is true, the American public diplomacy and strategic communication messages must constantly quote from recognized Islamic figures around the world who denounce the terrorists as unbelievers. (Some fatwa declarations, such as that of the Spanish Muslims in March, 2005, were squarely aimed at bin Laden and al Qaeda; others, including the British and American Muslim fatwas of July, 2005, did not.)[93]

Another means of branding the terrorists is to personalize the victims. A good branding campaign will show the photos, names, families and life stories cut short by radical Islamism – especially the victims killed by their own co-religionists and countrymen – constantly, relentlessly and graphically, especially in cultures unaccustomed to the heavily censored and sanitized images that appear in mainstream Western news sources. Terrorist propaganda videos in Iraq portray the innocent victims alongside the suicide bombers as martyrs.

The United States has not truly shown the world the horrible realities of militant Islamism. Many Arabic-language news services, by contrast, are extremely graphic. It is up to the U.S. to take the initiative and provide the needed context – and to do it with an immediacy that the cumbersome public affairs process thus far does not allow.

Use Only." The author posted the document on the Internet in 2005, at the following address: http://binladenquotes.blogspot.com.
[93] A senior State Department public diplomacy official, when presented with the Spanish fatwa idea as a missed opportunity, said that the department did not think the document important enough to translate and scoffed at the name of the individual who had raised the idea.

Branding the war

While branding the enemy, we also need to brand the war. A real war needs a real name that everyone can immediately recognize and understand. The name must:

- inspire confidence and unity of purpose, especially if the war is to be protracted;
- draw stark differences between both sides, unambiguously pitting the forces of good against the forces of evil;
- label the war's current nature or invoke the names of Good Fights of the past;
- have at its core an us-versus-them approach that leaves no doubt about the enemy and no room for neutrality;
- reinforce a sense of international togetherness against an unrelenting but defeatable foe; and
- inspire confidence and invincibility despite the promise of a long and bloody struggle and terrible sacrifice.

The name must be easy for ordinary people across cultures to understand. It must captivate the average citizen and make him part of the war effort, infusing the world with the sense of justice and solidarity.

The nation's greatest conflicts have had inspiring if sometimes varied names: American Revolution, Revolutionary War, or War of Independence; Civil War or War Between the States (depending on one's sympathies; some in the South prefer the more vivid War of Northern Aggression); the Great War of 1914-1918, as the cataclysmic conflict was called until the outbreak of the next great war, ultimately known as in the free world as World War II,[94] caused the Great War to become World War I.

Even the Korean war and Vietnam war, though not declared wars in the legal sense, provided a sense of geography and the idea of where the enemy was, as did the Mexican War, Indian wars, and the Spanish-American War in the nineteenth century. Interestingly,

---

[94] To this day in the Russian Federation, Stalin's brand-name for World War II – the "Great Patriotic War" – remains the popular and legal name. The branding is so deeply engrained in the Russian psyche that half the public continues to defend the Nazi-Soviet Pact of August, 1939, that precipitated the war.

those five geographically-themed wars are the least romanticized and often the most criticized of the nation's armed conflicts. The oddly named War of 1812 might evoke few passions from the average educated citizen today, but it burst with inspiration and romance, from the immortal "Don't Give Up the Ship" standard of the Battle of Lake Erie to Francis Scott Key's poem, penned on Baltimore harbor during a British naval bombardment, that became our national anthem. But looking too much at domestic precedents risks losing sight of the global audience.

The American label on the present war, either Global War on Terror or on Terrorism and dubbed GWOT (pronounced "GEE-wot") in Pentagon terminology, should pass as an interim name, just as the official name of the military response to 9/11, Operation Enduring Freedom, fell away as the war expanded.

Senior U.S. officials seemed to agree on the need for a GWOT name change by mid-2005, with some saying that the enemy is "extremism" and not necessarily terrorism. Some proposed a new name: War on Extremism, with the unfortunate acronym WOE.[95]

In 2006, administration officials contemplated not calling it a war after all. Instead, the conflict was a "struggle," specifically, a Struggle Against Violent Extremism (SAVE). By lowering the war footing to a mere struggle, advocates of the terminology change intended to send a message that the conflict was more than just military. Struggle, though, is anything but a decisive and confident-sounding term, especially in reference to a war effort led by the world's wealthiest and most militarily powerful nation. The defensive-sounding SAVE acronym also has Christian salvific connotations and needs no further comment.[96]

Some have proposed substituting "global" for "world" in a subtle and logical rhetorical shift to become the World War on Terror. But since the enemy is more the practitioners and sponsors of terror rather than the act itself, the name is unsatisfactory. A world war needs a number to follow it. Some argue for calling the current conflict World War III. This name brings back the sense of justice

---

[95] David Kaplan, "Sometimes, It's Just All in the Name," *US News & World Report*, June 6, 2005.

[96] The author's comments are not meant as criticism. Administration officials have been trying all along to come up with the answers to win the wars, while few opponents have offered constructive ideas to accomplish the mission more effectively.

and absolute good-versus-evil of World War II. But the name is sort of a letdown in some ways; for decades, in the popular mind, World War III was to have been a thermonuclear war between the superpowers. Even so, the Third World War is descriptive and unifying, yet general enough so that each of the allies can define the conflict as they must. Some who view the Cold War to have been a world war advocate a name change from GWOT to World War IV.[97]

Whatever its number, the "world war" term, say proponents, reduces the confusion about whether or not the war against Abu Sayyaf in the Philippines is part of the same conflict that brought about the bombings in London, Madrid and Bali, the riots in France, the war in Afghanistan, or the war in Iraq are connected with one another. In World War II, there was no mistaking that our troops in the Pacific were fighting the same war as our troops in North Africa, Asia, and Europe, even though Nazi Germany and Imperial Japan had little in common ideologically. U.S. leaders referred to each area of fighting as the "War in the Pacific" and "War in the Atlantic," but unmistakably as separate "theaters" or "fronts" of the same worldwide war. Even the most massive and protracted of fighting in one or two European countries or in and around Japan did not earn the official individual name "war." They were different "battles," wars in their own right, but still bloody parts of a much greater conflict.

President George W. Bush did refer to the U.S.-led invasions and occupations of Afghanistan and Iraq as "battles" in a global war. He specifically, if only briefly, mentioned what he called the "Battle of Afghanistan" and the "Battle of Iraq." However, the rest of the administration failed to follow, and soon the U.S. government and public as a whole defaulted back to the two-war position of the "Afghan War" and the "Iraq War," thus eliminating the message of connectedness between both conflicts as part of a larger global war against different enemies.

The name of the war should minimize the room for conflict among its very varied protagonists. The name should not try to define the universally undefinable term "terrorism," and it should not consider the enemy to be a methodology. Instead each protagonist should choose a definition of terrorism that best suits its own political and cultural climate, without ambiguity and fully implying international

---

[97] Credit for coining the term goes to Eliot A. Cohen, "World War IV: Let's Call This Conflict What It Is," *Wall Street Journal*, November 20, 2001.

solidarity. The accepted name for the war must provide wiggle room for complicated local situations, allowing individual national leaders to interpret the meaning as they must, permitting certain parties to see the light and switch from enemy to ally (as with Moscow in World War II) while presenting the broadest of fronts against the faceless enemy.

The name must put the people and bureaucracy on a war footing, presuming that the world is in mortal danger, while inspiring and uplifting people. A proper name accepts hardship and sacrifice against apparently insurmountable odds, marginalizes domestic defeatists and supporters of extremism who use the legal system to cripple the war effort, places mainstream war opponents on the defensive, and lends the unspoken assurance that in the end, if we all pull together, everything will be all right.

The Good Guys were the main victors in World Wars I and II, plus the Cold War which ended without the expected nuclear Armageddon. There is no reason, then, not to present an invincible front for the next generation or two until winning current World War III or IV. A speech by a distinguished national or international statesman, properly prepared and delivered, could educate the world and popularize the name.

Branding in Iraq

Through conviction and persistence, the U.S. effectively termed the 2003 invasion of Iraq a "liberation," though it has fought hard for its still incomplete, and waning, acceptance. The name of the mission, "Operation Iraqi Freedom," shaped the message unequivocally. (A review of American public diplomacy on Iraq is beyond the bounds of this chapter, though it must be said that the U.S. failed even to attempt to communicate strategically and persuasively with the world during the planning stages, thus undermining pro-U.S. leaders and political parties who wanted to help. The White House even dismissed the importance of talking points.[98])

---

[98] When this writer in August, 2002, asked the White House National Security Council press officer for talking points on the administration's goals in Iraq, the press officer told him that talking points were not necessary. Three days after this writer's story was published with the NSC's quote, the White House issued a set of talking points.

For our present purposes, we can see how the war produced its own crop of misused words that harmed the U.S. mission and inadvertently helped the enemy.

Even the clearest words and phrases can be misinterpreted, so it is again important to stress that messages be crafted to reinforce one another. A term for one part of the war effort must never conflict with, or detract from, the overall message of the war aim. One can also never presume that the words or phrases will translate faithfully into other languages or cultural contexts.

Neutrals and even advocates can misinterpret innocently; critics and adversaries can coin malicious translations or interpretations. This was true of Operation Iraqi Freedom. Legally, Iraq was not part of Operation Enduring Freedom, but the name implied a useful metaphor as a sub-conflict of the larger worldwide war.

At the same time, while obviously intended to inspire the troops, the Iraqi people and the rest of the world, the name of the operation inadvertently helped divert attention from the "war on terrorism" aspect of the conflict. The name reinforced not the GWOT message, but created a new tangent under a different set of reasons.

Consequently the idea that the "War in Iraq" was part of the Global War on Terror was a tough sell, especially with its absolutist weapons of mass destruction rationale. Apparently the result of lowest-common-denominator interagency negotiations, the WMD rationale never materialized in ways easy for the public to see and understand.

So what was the problem? The name of the operation needlessly opened itself to satire and worse, making it appear to validate enemy propaganda which portrayed the military action as an Anglo-American imperialist plot to steal Arab oil. While Saddam Hussein denounced the upcoming "war for oil," the White House was still fumbling with a coherent line. With much of the world predisposed to believe the worst about the British and Americans, Saddam's argument should have been expected to find ready believers. A peculiarity in the English language made the line even more plausible.

Here is where sensitivity to the nuances of culture comes into play: To London and Washington, Operation Iraqi Freedom (OIF) was an unmistakably positive name for the mission. However, it opened itself up to credible misinterpretation. In English, particularly American English, the words "freedom" and "liberty" are usually used interchangeably. Other languages have only one major word to describe the idea. "Freedom" has Anglo-Saxon origins, while "liberty" finds its roots in the Latin word *libertas*. Speakers of languages with even stronger Latin roots than English, use variations; in French, the preferred word is *liberté*.

It is logical and reasonable, then, for people of good or ill will to misunderstand or mistranslate Operation Iraqi Freedom as Operation Iraqi Liberty – with the unfortunate acronym OIL. Critics across the Internet passed along a false story that the Pentagon had originally chosen Operation Iraqi Liberty as the name of the invasion, but to avoid looking like a petroleum grab, had changed the word to "freedom." Aljazeera occasionally used the OIL abbreviation without comment, as did some mainline Western news organizations.

Saddam Hussein's line about American and coalition war aims, which a top Baghdad official presented to the United Nations in September, 2002, set the stage for the controversy that the subsequent OIF/OIL controversy reinforced. Some argue that fear of an American invasion for oil may have raised needless suspicions of Iraqis who otherwise might have supported or at least not opposed the coalition in its initial days and months. Since the "no war for oil" campaign had begun a half-year or more before the announcement of Operation Iraqi Freedom, senior U.S. officials would have had time to craft a name that would neither detract from the larger, worldwide war effort, nor reinforce the enemy's own propaganda.

But even the most allegedly wise sages of statecraft failed to take nuance seriously. Gilles Kepel of the Institute of Political Studies in Paris testified before the National Commission on Terrorist Attacks Upon the United States (the 9/11 Commission), saying that many Arabs thought that "the reason the armed operation was called Operation Iraqi Freedom and not Operation Iraqi Liberty was that the acronym for Operation Iraqi Liberty would have been O-I-L, and that O-I-F was more misleading."

The 9/11 commissioners failed to take the Frenchman's words to heart. Instead, according to the hearing transcript, the commissioners laughed.[99]

---

[99] See "Terrorism, Al Qaeda and the Muslim World," *Hearing on the National Commission on Terrorist Attacks Upon the United States*, July 9, 2003, typed transcript, pp. 82-83.

Branding the enemy in Iraq

The U.S. very effectively demonized the initial enemy in Iraq – the regime of Saddam Hussein and the ruling Ba'athist party – well before the fighting began. Once the regime had collapsed, however, the U.S. leaders did not brand the new enemies who emerged, even though those enemies proved more resilient and deadly than the Ba'athist power structure.

Several months after the liberation, when coalition forces announced the transition from invasion to counterinsurgency, the U.S. military officially designated the new enemy in Iraq: Insurgents. From a purely military perspective, the term is accurate. From political and psychological approaches, the term is inadequate and even misleading. The value-neutral word "insurgent" sanitizes the enemy of its terroristic nature, given that the enemy's main targets are no longer merely foreign occupation forces, but the Iraqi people themselves. The technical term retains the possibility that the entire insurgency is legitimate.

The new enemy was as bad or worse than the toppled regime, yet the coalition offered only a small vilification campaign outside the Iraqi theater, despite the perfection of the circumstances. As its modus operandi, the enemy was targeting mosques, churches, streets, shops, markets, government officials, clergymen, local citizens seeking employment to rebuild their country and feed their families, even children excitedly taking candy from American soldiers: perfect examples of the work of mufsidoon evildoers. The attacks outdid one another in the absoluteness of their evil, going beyond the targeting of women and children to sending children to die as unwitting props in bomb-filled automobiles.

Journalists and public figures, even official spokesmen, have given the "insurgents" dozens of other names – many of which are incomplete or otherwise misleading. Some are wildly inaccurate or even dishonest, conferring legitimacy and even virtue. Labels include: activists, agitators, anti-Americans, anti-Iraqi forces, former Ba'athists, Ba'athist holdovers, Ba'athist remnants, criminals, criminal gangs, dead-enders, *fedayeen* (a praiseworthy and thus inappropriate term), former regime members, fringe groups, fundamentalists, guerrillas, insurgents, martyrs, militants, muj, mujahidin, paramilitaries, radicals, regime loyalists, resistance fighters, renegades, rogue elements, Saddam elements, Saddam followers, Sunni extremists, unlawful combatants, and of course, jihadis and jihadists.[100]

If the government and news media can introduce Arabic words like jihad into official and public discourse and incorporate them into the English language, certainly they can do the same with concepts like mufsidoon. All it takes is persistence in daily press briefings and public statements.

Lessons for shaping the "brand" message

We conclude, then, with lessons for shaping the American and allied message through effective branding:

- Do no harm except to the enemy's image and ego. Never help the enemy enhance his prestige among his followers and wound-be followers;
- Recapture the language;
- Always craft messages that diminish the enemy's reputation, especially within his own camp;
- The most effective attacks on the enemy's reputation are often from recognized figures within the enemy's own community, and not necessarily from official U.S. pronouncements;
- Never brand the enemy in ways that diminish the American presidency or the United States government in general;
- Do not play into the enemy's hands by making him look larger than life or invincible;
- Coin the name of the conflict at your own initiative and on your own terms;
- Choose a name that stirs people's emotions and imagination, cross-culturally when possible;
- Demonize the enemy using the enemy's own words and actions against him;
- Ensure that the themes never conflict with or diverge from one another, and make them reinforce one another; and
- Be consistent and persistent to the point of being relentless.

---

[100] And then there are the U.S.-centric labels like "foreigners" and "foreign fighters" in Iraq, terms that sound odd to anyone outside the United States, to say nothing of the Iraqi people, who also view American forces as foreigners. The author thanks Jim Guirard, who developed most of the above list in a larger compilation from press reports and official statements.

None of this is difficult. All of it has been done before, and some in and out of uniform are doing it today. The only missing ingredient is the political will to do it worldwide and do it consistently.

5

The secret weapon
that's worse than death

Introduction

Demonization of the enemy is the general default position of American message-making against international threats, but it can go only so far. The history of warfare shows that while demonization can build and maintain alliances and coalitions, and is important to maintain national unity in a protracted conflict, demonization can inadvertently aid the enemy's own war aims.

Incessant, morbid portrayals of an individual, movement, or nation as a mortal enemy might rally support for the American side, but the messages often have a shelf-life that gets tired as the conflict stretches out. Constant specters of unrelenting dangers risk sowing defeatism and chipping away at our own morale. Overdoing the specter of the threat risks making the U.S. look like a bully in some places and surrenders the propaganda advantage to the other side. Too much demonization can also help brand the enemy in ways contrary to U.S. interests. Appearing to call "wolf" too often can also cause cynicism at home and distrust abroad. The questions at this stage of the war are:

- Do we inadvertently aid our enemies and potential enemies by taking them too seriously?
- Does our relentless portrayal of individuals, ideologies, movements and philosophies as mortal dangers to America

diminish the stature of the U.S. or enhance the enemies' status and prestige?

- Is it an unsound political strategy to hype the image and power of the enemy and the few leaders who personify it?
- Is there something else the United States and its allies should be doing in their attempts to discredit, undermine and defeat the enemy?

The answer is "yes" to all of the above. In this chapter, we suggest that U.S. strategy includes undermining the political and psychological strengths of adversaries and enemies by employing ridicule and satire as standard operating tools of strategic communication. Ridicule is an under-appreciated weapon not only against terrorists, but against weapons proliferators, despots, and international undesirables in general. Ridicule serves several purposes:

- Ridicule raises morale at home;
- Ridicule strips the enemy/adversary of his mystique and prestige;
- Ridicule erodes the enemy's claim to justice;
- Ridicule deprives the enemy of his ability to terrorize;
- Ridicule eliminates the enemy's image of invincibility; and
- Directed properly at an enemy, ridicule can be a fate worse than death.

The power of ridicule

Used as a means of positive persuasion, humor can be an important public diplomacy tool. "If I can get you to laugh with me," said comedian John Cleese of Monty Python fame, "you like me better, which makes you more open to my ideas. And if I can persuade you to laugh at the particular point I make, by laughing at it you acknowledge the truth."[101] Humor is an excellent means of making policy points and building constructive relations abroad. Everybody wins.

Laughing *at* someone – ridicule – is another matter. It is the use of humor at someone else's expense. It is a zero-sum game destructive

---

[101] Harry Mills, *Artful Persuasion* (American Management Association, 2000), p. 131.

to one of the parties involved. Like a gun, ridicule is a dangerous weapon. Even in trained hands, it can misfire. Used carelessly or indiscriminately, ridicule can create enemies were there were none, and deepen hostilities among the very peoples whom the user seeks to win over.

That said, in nearly every aspect of society and across cultures and time, ridicule works. Ridicule leverages the emotions and simplifies the complicated and takes on the powerful, in politics, business, law, entertainment, the media, literature, culture, sports and romance. Ridicule can tear down faster than the other side can rebuild. It can smash a theoretical or intellectual construct. A target might counter an argument, an image, or even a kinetic force, but he can marshal few defenses against the well-aimed barbs that bleed humiliation and spawn contempt.

Politicians fear ridicule. Some take ridicule well and emerge stronger for it; others never recover. The perpetual circle of democracy absorbs and even breeds ridicule against individuals and ideas, while the system itself remains intact. While ridicule can be a healthy part of democracy, it can weaken the tyrant.

The ancients and ridicule

We get the word "satire" from the ancient Greek *satyr*, the mythical drunk, hedonistic or otherwise naughty man-goat. Satyrs performed the fourth and final part of a tetralogy drama, usually in a burlesque performance that poked fun at the preceding serious or tragic trilogy. The audience would leave the performance satisfied and upbeat.

Prominent Classical literary figures used satire and ridicule against war. Poet-playwright Aristophanes, for example, in 425 B.C., satirized Athenian policy of the Peloponnesian War in *The Acharnians*, and mocked government, society and war in subsequent plays; he filled his plays with invective and *ad hominem* attacks as well as sexual humor.

Aristophanes' barbed ribaldry notwithstanding, Greek society, irrespective of the type of government, placed boundaries on the types and intensity of ridicule. Other classical societies did, as well. While permitted under certain circumstances, ridicule was seen as such a devastatingly powerful weapon that the ancients proscribed its use except in extreme situations. Political humor troubled Augustus Caesar to the point that he banned jokes about the Roman emperor. In Christianity, ridicule of another person is considered uncharitable and can even be sinful, except, one can argue, in time of war when violence and killing can be morally permissible, or to avert or shorten a military conflict.[102]

In the Talmud, the basis of Jewish law, the ancient Hebrews proclaimed, "All mockery (*leitzanut*) is prohibited except for mockery of idol worship (*avoday zarah*)," mockery being so destructive it can be used only against evil.[103]

Muhammad, the founder of Islam, personally used ridicule as a weapon of war early after he announced his prophethood.[104] Islamic poets were not mere literary artists; they were often warriors who wrote satire and ridicule of the enemy as an important weapon of offensive warfare. Muhammad banned the faithful from drawing human images, including his own, in large part to stamp out idolatry. But he promoted the use of humiliation as a weapon and as an instrument of justice. The violence of Muslim overreactions in early 2006 to some European cartoons depicting Muhammad appear to be manifestations of the vulnerability to the power of ridicule than truly offended sensitivities.[105]

As we saw earlier, in Islamic tradition punishment for hirabah could include dismemberment for the purpose of humiliating the offender.[106] Extreme Islamists equate ridicule with pain and even

---

[102] The author hopes that this book will help open up a moral debate on the just use of ridicule and other forms of political and psychological warfare as instruments of statecraft.

[103] Rabbi Uri Cohen, "Balak – God's Laughter: Making Fun of Balaam," *Nishmat*, Jerusalem Center for Advanced Study of Jewish Women, accessed January 18, 2006. Rabbi Cohen, a professor at Princeton University, is also a stand-up comedian.

[104] Chronology of Islam, Canadian Society of Muslims (Toronto) http://muslim-canada.org/chronol.htm

[105] Were one to use cartoons against Islamist extremists, one would seek to marginalize the extremists from their support base and from the rest of Islam. The cartoonist would make the extremists' own appearance and behavior the object of ridicule, and never the Islamic religion or the prophet themselves. In addition to betraying the principles of freedom of religion and respect for other religions, making fun of another's religion is counterproductive to the war effort.

[106] Sherman A. Jackson (a.k.a. Abdul Hakim), "Domestic Terrorism in the Islamic Legal Tradition," *Muslim World*, Vol. 91, No. 3-4, Fall 2001, pp. 293-310. Also see, Sayyid M. Syeed, letter to Jim Guirard, cited by

death.[107] Bin Laden has said that he fears humiliation more than death itself.[108]

Tyrants, terrorists and ridicule

Dictators, tyrants, and those aspire to seize and keep power by intimidation and force can tolerate no public ridicule. They generally harbor grandiose self-images with little bearing on how people really think of them. They require a controlled political environment, reinforced by sycophants and toadies, to preserve an impenetrable image. Some are more tolerant of reasoned or principled opposition but few of satire or ridicule. The size of their egos may be seen as inversely proportional to the thickness of their skin. Knowing of then-dictator Manuel Noriega's acute sensitivity to mockery about his acne scars, the Panamanian opposition likened his face to a pineapple and used the fruit as a symbol of resistance.

Few dictators are true madmen; most are rational and serious.[109] Saddam Hussein had a strong sense of humor, and is known to have told mildly self-deprecating stories about himself in public.[110] That is not to say he accepted others' stories; Saddam's storytelling was under his own control.

Hence the vulnerability: Control is the essence of an authoritarian movement or dictatorship. Jokes and contempt know no philosophy and a good laugh, even of the gallows humor variety, is almost impossible to control when spread virally.

Russian émigré comedian Yakov Smirnov often referred to the Soviet government's "Department of Jokes" that censored all spoken

---

Guirard, "Properly Condemning the al Qaeda Blasphemy," *The American Muslim*, April 21, 2003.

[107] Aboud al-Zumur, Jama'at al-Jihad al-Islami (The Methodology of the Islamic Jihad Group), written at Turah Penitentiary, Cairo, Egypt, 1986. Translation by U.S. Department of State.

[108] Bin Laden said in January, 2006: "I swear not to die but a free man even if I taste the bitterness of death. I fear to be humiliated or betrayed." BBC, "Text: 'Bin Laden Tape,'" January 19, 2006, 21:53 GMT, http://news.bbc.co.uk/2/hi/middle_east/4628932.stm.

[109] See Jerrold M. Post, *Leaders and their Followers in a Dangerous World: The Psychology of Political Behavior* (Cornell University Press, 2004).

[110] Mark Bowden, "Tales of the Tyrant," *The Atlantic*, May 2002, pp. 36-37.

and written humor. While we have found no evidence of a Soviet unit with that specific name, we do know that the Communist Party Central Committee's Propaganda Department and the KGB Fifth Chief Directorate respectively set and enforced ideological discipline in which a "Department of Jokes" or its equivalent would reside.

"No great movement designed to change the world can bear to be laughed at or belittled," Czechoslovakian novelist Milan Kundera wrote in *The Joke*, "because laughter is the rust that corrodes every thing."[111]

Fidel Castro understood the principle when, six months after seizing power in 1959, he ordered signs placed in all official buildings that read, "Counter-revolutionary jokes forbidden here." One of the first Cuban publications that Castro shut down was *Zig Zag*, a magazine of humor.[112]

While the Russians ultimately did away with a department of jokes, their president, Boris Yeltsin, could laugh at his political opponents' innovative, irreverent and wildly popular political satire TV puppet show, *Kukly*. But the sense of humor of his tough-minded successor, former KGB Lt. Col. Vladimir Putin, allows no such ability. Putin shut down *Kukly* and the NTV television channel that produced it. In Putin's Russia, mocking or insulting the president is a crime punishable by imprisonment. Venezuelan strongman Hugo Chavez pushed through a similar law to protect himself from open ridicule and expressions of disrespect.

In the 1980s, the Islamic Republic of Iran went so far as to assassinate jokesters abroad, even in western Europe, where the regime murdered an exiled humorist in Germany and a London merchant who sold CD recordings that mocked the mullahs. In today's Iran, friends take taxi rides just to share jokes away from informers in their schools and workplaces.

Repression cannot stamp out humor. In the words of Professor Luis Aguilar of Georgetown University, repression "only drives it underground. For repressed people, [humor] is a subtle form of

---

[111] Milan Kundera, *The Joke*, trans. Henry Heim (Harper & Row, 1984). The author acknowledges writer Ben MacIntyre for locating the Kundera reference and others in his column, "Saddam Has Only Got One Ball," *The Times*, 26 August 2005, p. 24.

[112] Luis E. Aguilar, *"Chistes" – Political Humor in Cuba* (Cuban-American National Foundation, 1989), p. i.

rebellion; a collective means to pay back the oppressor; the last resort; the last laugh."[113]

Empowering the powerless

That collective payback, that last laugh, can empower the powerless. It need not be expressed outwardly, where doing so could mean punishment or even death. Even in the most repressive societies, quiet or inward expression remains alive, ready to flame with the first breath of oxygen. Jokes are a release of the fearful, a rewarding act of defiance, a rhetorical rock hurled at the oppressor. The best ones spread because they speak the truth, and the truth leads to freedom. The joke is quietly shared and spread; the people know that they are not alone. "Every joke is a tiny revolution," said George Orwell. "Whatever destroys dignity, and brings down the mighty from their seats, preferably with a bump, is funny."[114]

Ridicule as an offensive weapon

Like rifles and satellites, submarines and propaganda, ridicule is a neutral piece of technology. It can soften up entrenched and hardened targets, especially when those targets have alienated large parts of the population, or even small but loud elements in society.

French revolutionaries preceded their overthrow and murder of the king and his family through relentless campaigns of ridicule in the rather politically-open society of late 18th century Paris. Constant, vicious, often crude parody and mockery of the king as an individual and the monarchy as a system, as well as the aristocracy and the Church, arguably motivated and radicalized the public more than the high-minded philosophies of the revolutionaries.

Combined with positive philosophical, reasoned and inspiring campaigns of *Liberté, Egalité, Fraternité*, the abuse stripped away the moral legitimacy the monarchy had from the outwardly respectful French subjects, and made the king the butt of constant sexual and scatological humor that, along with the excesses of the time, reduced the monarchy in many French eyes to a contemptible

---

[113] Ibid.

[114] George Orwell, "Funny, but Not Vulgar," *Leader*, 28 July 1945, in Sonia Orwell and Ian Angus, eds., *Orwell: As I Please, 1943-1945, The Collected Essays, Journals and Letters* (Nonpareil, 2000), pp. 283-288.

canker that deserved and cried out for destruction. Popular history remembers the pious Marie Antoinette as her French executioners caricatured her.

Mass murderers can still have a good laugh, but usually at others' expense. Adolf Hitler's sense of humor knew no self-deprecation; his was what the Germans call *schadenfreude*, a word that has no English equivalent but can be understood as taking malicious pleasure at others' misfortune. Hitler loved cruel jokes on his own ministers, especially on Foreign Minister Ribbentrop,[115] but always away from public view. He could not laugh at himself. His propagandists in 1933 tried to appeal to the satirical-minded German public by issuing a compendium of tame political cartoons, but the effort went nowhere.

The Nazis and fascists required either adulation or fear. That requirement made their leaders and their causes vulnerable to well-aimed ridicule. Hitler with his Charlie Chaplin-style toothbrush mustache (a former aide later said it made him look like he had a cold), his uniform-loving Hermann Goering, and his club-footed propaganda chief Joseph Goebbels made great caricatures of their own. So did the flamboyant Benito Mussolini, who rehearsed his oratorical gesticulations – which could be impressive in person or on film, but made to look silly in still frames – before a mirror. German jokes about the Nazis quickly went underground, but resurfaced when the people saw the regime near collapse toward the end of the war.

Ridicule as a defensive weapon

Little if any American World War II-era ridicule had much effect on continental Europe, but it was still vital to the war effort at home. Ridicule can be a defensive weapon if it helps calm the fears of the public at home and give hope that they can indeed defeat the enemy. British and American boys sang anti-Hitler songs, sometimes mocking the fuehrer's private parts and what Mussolini did with them, as one might expect from adolescents. Laughing at the enemy during wartime helps one become less fearful and more optimistic of victory.

Popular culture also mocked the Axis powers – not after a decent interval following a given incident or atrocity, but from the start.

---

[115] Albert Speer, *Inside the Third Reich* (Simon & Schuster, 1970).

The Three Stooges, one of the most popular comic groups in cinema at the time, performed the first parodies of the enemy in 1940. Moe made ridiculous slapstick impressions of Hitler. Larry heiled as propaganda minister, and Curly dressed as Goering with his belly and buttocks festooned with medals. Moe also impersonated a laughable Tojo. One episode poked fun at Stalin. Others in Hollywood also helped the war effort through humor and ridicule. Charlie Chaplin's famous full-length movie, *The Great Dictator*, though developed years before, followed the first Stooges episode in 1940. Chaplin – complaining that Hitler had stolen his trademark mustache – starred as fuehrer lookalike Adenoid Hynkel, accompanied by his sidekick Benzoni Napolini, dictator of Bacteria.

Like many in Hollywood did at the time, the cartoon studios put their talent at the disposal of the war effort. Disney's Donald Duck, in the 1942 short "Donald Duck In Nutziland" (retitled "Der Fuehrer's Face"), dreamed he was stuck in Nazi Germany. The cartoon won an Academy Award. Disney produced dozens of anti-Axis cartoons, as did Warner Bros. starring Bugs Bunny and Daffy Duck. Both studios have released some of the cartoon shorts on video but limited the rebroadcast and banned the re-release of some on what critics call political correctness grounds.[116]

The United States occasionally used ridicule and satire in film to influence elections abroad. Large-scale American intervention in Italy's 1948 election, in which the Communist Party was believed able to win a parliamentary plurality, saved the day for the Christian Democrats. Among the many instruments the U.S. used to convince Italians to vote against the Communist Popular Front was the romantic comedy *Ninotchka*, a parody of life in the Soviet Union starring Greta Garbo and Melvyn Douglas.[117] "This film, which hilariously satirized life in Russia, tended to leave an audience with a feeling that if this is Russia please deliver us from such a society," one observer reported. "Distributors provided double the usual number of copies of the film, and special arrangements were made so that the film would be shown immediately among the low-income-level population."

---

[116] *Bugs & Daffy Wartime Cartoons* (Warner Bros., 1942-45; released on VHS video, 1998); *Walt Disney Treasures – On the Front Lines* (Disney DVD, 2004).

[117] *Ninotchka* (MGM, 1939; Warner Home Video DVD, 2005).

The film was so effective that the Italian Communists tried to prevent it from being shown; after the Italians voted against the Communists, one party worker complained, "What licked us was *Ninotchka*."[118]

Current anti-terrorist ridicule that worries little of political correctness is *Team America: World Police*, a clever animated marionette show about a covert counterterrorism force that patriotically if clumsily fights Islamist terrorists and North Korean dictator Kim Jong-il.[119] Conceptually, *Team America* is an effective example of parody that plays on the obvious faults of an insecure and lonely Kim, the absurdity of United Nations diplomacy in the person of weapons inspector Hans Blix, and on popular stereotypes about Islamist terrorists and Hollywood anti-war personalities.

Developed by the creators of the South Park cartoon, *Team America* limits its effectiveness, as well as the size of its audience, with extremely crude adolescent (some might call it "adult") humor. Even cleaned up, the movie's style and sense of humor might not be effective in other cultures.[120] Nevertheless, *Team America* is a masterpiece of over-the-top ridicule that could be to the current young generation what the irreverent *Monty Python and the Holy Grail* was to young people thirty years ago. *Team America* puts the bad guys in their place and shows that, as clumsy and arrogant as Americans might be to many people, they are still the good guys. Such movies might reinforce domestic morale and reduce the fear of our enemies. For example, few Americans prior to *Team America* would think to laugh at Kim Jong-il.

Ridicule and U.S. strategy

Americans have used ridicule as a potent weapon to cut its enemies down to size since the Revolutionary War. Ridicule has

---

[118] See William E. Daugherty and Morris Janowitz, eds., *A Psychological Warfare Casebook* (Johns Hopkins University Press, 1958).

[119] *Team America: World Police* (Paramount DVD, 2005).

[120] One must not discount the value of adolescent humor in winning the war of ideas. While many find it patently offensive, such humor can appeal to adolescent boys and young men unlike any other form of propaganda, and by its nature is self-replicating. In the global war of ideas, the young male demographic is one of the most important, yet impenetrable to date, markets for counterterrorism strategists. The key is to develop culturally nuanced adolescent humor that resonates within a specific targeted society.

long served two wartime purposes: to raise the people's morale by helping them to laugh at their enemies, and to dent the morale of enemy forces. Despite their far superior training, discipline, skill and firepower, the British were unprepared for combat with the colonists. The Americans were guerrilla fighters who had the bad form not to stand in formation on a battlefield, and to shoot at enemy officers.

The British handily won the first engagement, the Battle of Lexington in April, 1775, but suffered heavy losses during their march from Concord back to Boston with Americans shooting at them from behind trees and rocks. Bostonians jeered. Among the many poems and ditties circulating around Boston after the opening shots of the war at Lexington and Concord was this one:

> *How brave you went out with muskets all bright,*
> *And thought to befrighten the folks with the sight;*
> *But when you got there how they powder'd your pums,*
> *And all the way home how they pepper'd your bums,*
> *And is it not, honies, a comical farce,*
> *To be proud in the face, and be shot in the arse.*[121]

Such mockery stung. The British army at the time was the finest, most experienced and most formidable in the world, its officers and men proud of their history of what they viewed as gentlemanly warfighting. The practically un-trained, mostly un-uniformed, often un-disciplined, frequently uncouth, and generally low-class American riffraff, in British eyes, were no worthy adversary at all.

With fife and drum as important means of battlefield coordination and communication, British troops ridiculed the Americans with songs like "Yankee Doodle," whose mocking lyrics the colonists changed and embraced as their own anthem. That counter-ridicule operation unsettled the Redcoats. One British soldier recorded, "After our rapid successes, we held the Yankees in great contempt, but it was not a little mortifying to hear them play this tune."[122]

Local patriots heaped abuse on British civilian and military officials. They directed a poem at General William Howe, whom

---

[121] Philip M. Taylor, *Munitions of the Mind* (Manchester University Press, 2003), p. 135.
[122] Ibid.

George III had named royal military governor of Massachusetts in the winter of 1775, and at Howe's mistress, Mrs. Joshua Loring:

Sir William, he, snug as a flea,
Lay all this time a-snoring
Nor dreamed of harm, as he lay warm
In bed with Mrs. -------.[123]

Benjamin Franklin was famous in the colonies and Europe as a colorful humorist as well as inventor and scientist. As a colonial agent in London, he used humor to win sympathy for the colonies' grievances, and tried persuasion through gentle satire, such as his 1773 essay on "Rules by Which a Great Empire May Be Reduced to a Small One," a blueprint that showed how, through poor treatment of its colonies, the British government was destroying its imperium.

Franklin at the time viewed himself as an Englishman from Pennsylvania, and did not support the idea of American independence. Soon that would change. He used ridicule as a weapon at home as a printer, writer and patriot, and later in France as a diplomat, propagandist and intelligence officer.

Ridicule for today's conflicts

With the proliferation of communications technology, ridicule is a cheap and easy way to wage conflicts short of war, or to undermine an enemy in time of war. Thin-skinned dictators include Castro of Cuba, Kim Jong-il of North Korea, Alexander Lukashenko of Belarus, Hugo Chavez of Venezuela, and the regimes of China, Vietnam, and many predominantly Muslim countries. The more autocratic or extreme the leader, the more vulnerable he is to ridicule.

Being a declared adversary – even enemy – of the United States is a status symbol among the world's terrorists, dictators, and political extremists. By taking that enemy too seriously, by hyping it up as a threat, the United States is unintentionally credentializing a heretofore insignificant individual or group, and giving it the stature it needs to rise above its own society, establish itself, attract recruits, and gain influence. Ridicule can cut the enemy down to size.

---

[123] A. J. Langguth, *Patriots: The Men Who Started the American Revolution* (Simon & Schuster, 1988), p. 313.

Arab, Persian and other predominantly Islamic cultures have long traditions of using ridicule for political and military purposes, presenting the U.S. with ample opportunities. The practice of militaristic ridicule dates from the third- to fifth years of Muhammad's annunciation as prophet, when he employed ridicule aggressively against enemies, ahead of his invading forces.

Poets wrote not so much for entertainment or storytelling as for psychological purposes to help achieve military ends. The popularity of some medieval Arab poets has been undergoing a revival since the 1980s, where the most extreme have provided intellectual and ideological foundations for Wahhabi and Salafi brands of militant Islamism and their terrorist manifestations.

Muslims around the world have ridiculed Islamist extremists and their terroristic interpretations of the Qur'an as few American writers, comedians and broadcasters would ever dare. Pakistani TV has run shows mocking the extremists. A popular Iraqi comedian made fun of all parties in his country's conflict, only to be assassinated in late 2006 by the "insurgents." Political satire in literature, music and movies are some of the biggest sellers in the Arabic-speaking markets. Arab, Iranian and Indonesian stand-up comics already perform stinging political satire across the world, but few are well-known and even fewer have outlets, though if they were "discovered" their listenership could be in the hundreds of millions.

The previous Iranian government tolerated some forms of political satire, but Iran's top political impersonator Ali Dean, who did hilarious impressions of various mullahs, was forced to an American exile. Private Farsi-language TV stations in North America lampoon Iranian leaders. The most influential station, NITV, is owned by an exiled Iranian rock star, with Dean as its top humorist, broadcasting into Iran and with no U.S. government support.[124]

In his California exile from Iran, Ali Dean studies the mullahs' sermons and speeches for his material. "They hate me because they don't like [anybody to] impersonate them," he says. "To them, they are untouchable. To me, there is no untouchable."[125]

Making a terrorist look like a fool

---

[124] Author's interview with Zia Atabay, President, NITV, July, 2003.
[125] Bob Simon, "Lights, Camera, Revolution," CBS News, 18 June 2003.

Meanwhile, we are faced with the challenge of taking down elusive terrorist targets that we cannot find or defeat physically.

An excellent case study of U.S. forces using ridicule in the present day is the release of an unedited video of the al Qaeda chief in Iraq, Abu Musab al-Zarqawi, in 2006. Zarqawi had controlled his entire public persona through making and releasing videos of himself. The Jordanian-born terrorist tried to portray himself as an invincible Muslim warrior, either masked while beheading an unarmed captive, or wearing a black "uniform" and firing an automatic weapon. After a long and painstaking hunt, the U.S. military killed Zarqawi on June 8, 2006.

Zarqawi's rigid control of his public image was also a vulnerability. Like the Wizard of Oz, who lost his ability to instill fear after a dog pulled away a curtain to expose a little man in a booth, extremists who depend on controlling their images can lose their authority quickly if they are exposed.

The terrorist's last video, posted on the Internet on April 25, 2006, showed him in the desert firing a captured American machine gun and acting authoritative and in control. U.S. forces captured the unedited original, apparently prior to the Internet posting. The raw original depicted the al Qaeda leader in a very different fashion. On May 4, Maj. Gen. Rick Lynch, a spokesman for the U.S. Command in Baghdad, presented the edited and raw videos to the press, along with commentary about Zarqawi's competence as a real warrior.

In showing the edited video, Lynch commented how Zarqawi was "very proud of the fact that he can operate this machine gun, and he proclaims that, and all of his close associates are very proud of what Zarqawi does." Then Lynch displayed the captured unedited video, in which Zarqawi found his weapon jammed and was unable to clear it without help. "It's supposed to be automatic fire. He's shooting single shots," said Lynch. "Something is wrong with his machine gun. He looks down, can't figure it out, calls his friend to come unblock the stoppage and get the weapon firing again."

The general then narrated the rest of the video: "This piece you all see as he walks away, he's wearing his black uniform and his New Balance tennis shoes as he moves to this white pickup. And his close associates around him ... do things like grab the hot barrel of the machine gun and burn themselves."[126]

---

[126] "U.S. Shows Previously Unseen al-Zarqawi Video," Associated Press, May 4, 2006, variations with updates throughout the day.

This writer viewed the news conference and noted the positive reaction from the assembled journalists, including non-U.S. journalists. Immediate news coverage was positive, with television channels and websites showing the still footage and displaying the videos. Iraqi television repeatedly broadcast the briefing and the mockery of Zarqawi. Aljazeera played down the briefing and did not air the video itself. This contrast is enough to show how the message resonated among Arabic-speaking audiences.

An Arab reporter for the Associated Press, in a story carried around the world, began with this lead: "Abu Musab al-Zarqawi is shown wearing American tennis shoes and unable to operate his automatic rifle in video released Thursday by the U.S. military as part of a propaganda war aimed at undercutting the image of the terror leader." AP reported that Lynch "mocked al-Zarqawi as the previously unseen footage showed a smiling al-Qaeda leader first firing single shots from a U.S.-made M-249 light machine gun. A frown creeps across al-Zarqawi's face as the weapon appears to jam. He looks at the rifle, confused, then summons another fighter." [127]

AP quoted Gen. Lynch and added its own commentary: "By contrast, the edited version which the militants posted on the Web showed what happened only after the fighter fixed the weapon – a fierce-looking al-Zarqawi confidently blasting away with bursts of automatic gunfire. His fellow fighters and associates appear similarly inept in the newly released footage. One reaches out to grab a just-fired weapon by the barrel, apparently unaware that it would burn his hand." [128]

By every reasonable measure, the briefing was a success. The U.S. had cut its elusive foe down to size and won a full news cycle's worth of positive press that severely degraded the image of the enemy. Friendly Arab TV loved it. A problem remained, however. If Zarqawi was so inept, why couldn't the U.S. and Coalition forces find him? This was a tough question that the public affairs officers appeared not to anticipate. Follow-on reporting and media commentary asked that question, which reflected badly on the military. Indeed, many thought that the U.S. looked foolish for not being able to hunt down such a pathetic adversary. Public affairs officers pronounced the ridicule briefing to have been an

---

[127] Tarek Al-Tablawi, "Video Shows Al-Zarqawi Fumbling with Rifle," Associated Press, May 4, 2006, updated 6:53 p.m. Eastern.
[128] Ibid.

embarrassment to the armed forces and later quashed attempts on the information operations front to cast ridicule and scorn on the insurgents and terrorists. Coincidentally, Maj. Gen. Lynch's May 4 briefing disappeared from the Pentagon's defenselink.mil website.

The mistake, however, was not to take down Zarqawi's image a few notches. The mistake was to have played into the terrorists' hands from the beginning by portraying him as larger than life. That was a strategic error from public affairs and other message-makers. The Zarqawi video is a helpful example to demonstrate what to do correctly (use intelligence to attack the enemy's image) and what not to do (craft an image strategy that makes the enemy look invincible), in order to avoid making oneself look ridiculous.

But even then, had the Coalition been proactive rather than reactive, it could have responded effectively to negative media comments about the Coalition's inability to capture Zarqawi using ridicule. For example, message-makers could have suggested that he was able to avoid capture only by hiding with the women, perhaps even dressing like one, thereby showing that he was not worthy of admiration or emulation. Public affairs could have pointed out that he was willing to send out others to fight because he was too cowardly to do so himself. The video could have been used again to support the assertion that the only time he was willing to be filmed was when firing a weapon miles from the nearest American or when killing a bound and blindfolded unarmed civilian. Washington-based officials and PAOs in-theater lacked the detailed knowledge and situational awareness to understand that such strategies can work and were too timid to implement such an aggressive and controversial approach to begin with. So they did nothing, and when some bright and assertive people took an opportunity, the PAOs ran away.

Another example of political correctness and ignorance with regard to the value of ridicule occurred when U.S. Special Operations Command (SOCOM) was unable to secure higher level approval for the deployment of a cartoon based on the concept of three bumbling terrorists who continually failed to achieve their mission. This concept, a combination of the Road Runner cartoon series and the Three Stooges, tested well with Muslim audiences who found the satire to diminish their own images of the terrorists. SOCOM, however, never aired the programming.

U.S. policymakers must incorporate ridicule into their strategic thinking. Ridicule is a tool that they can use without having to micromanage. It exists naturally in its native environments in ways beneficial to the interests of the nation and cause of freedom. Its practitioners are natural allies, even if we do not always appreciate what they say or how they say it. The United States need do little more than give them publicity and play on its official and semi-official global radio, TV and Internet media, and help them become "discovered." And the U.S. should be relentless about it.

Conclusion

Ridicule is a powerful weapon of warfare. It can be a strategic weapon. The United States must take advantage of it against terrorists, proliferators, and other threats. Ridicule is vital because:

- It sticks;
- The target can't refute it;
- It is almost impossible to repress, even if driven underground;
- It spreads on its own and multiplies naturally;
- It can get better with each re-telling;
- It boosts morale at home;
- Our enemy shows far greater intolerance to ridicule than we;
- Ridicule divides the enemy, damages its morale, and makes it less attractive to supporters and prospective recruits; and
- The ridicule-armed warrior need not fix a physical sight on the target. Ridicule will find its own way to the targeted individual. To the enemy, being ridiculed means losing respect. It means losing influence. It means losing followers and repelling potential new backers.

To the enemy, ridicule can be worse than death. Many of our enemies believe death to be a supernatural martyrdom. Ridicule is much worse: defeat without martyrdom, the worst of both worlds. And they have to live with it.

6

Spectrum of messages

Introduction

America's audience spans an immense spectrum across most of the world – not just Muslims. While some messages can have a near-universal effect, many will resonate only in certain cultural contexts, or even only with sub-spectra or microcultures. Some audiences are ready and in want of positive American messages; others are unwilling or unready to receive or accept positive messages about the United States, but would accept negative messages about the enemy.

For cultural reasons concerning the framing and delivery of messages, the world audiences on matters of Islamist extremism may be divided between the ummah of Muslim believers where the actual ideological conflict is taking place, and non-Muslim societies. On issues apart from Islamist terrorism, the cultural divides are less of a factor for the message-maker and is not a consideration for the purposes of this present discussion.

The U.S. has been pursuing many of the issues explored in this chapter, with varying degrees of success in localized areas, but not on an integrated, global scale as a matter of national strategy. In this chapter, we will:

- Discuss the diverse nature of our world audience, and define principal near-term message targets;
- Develop message strategies to divide terrorists and extremists from their popular support bases;
- Develop message strategies to divide terrorists and extremists from one another;

- Expand a splittist message strategy to marginalize and isolate extremists and their sympathizers, discredit them, and destroy their effectiveness to operate and recruit;
- Carry that message strategy further to expand the universe of people likely to work against the extremists;
- Study an important authoritative fatwa or Islamic legal and religious decision that provides an important model for message-makers to aid the war effort.

We will first approach the nature and tone of the ideological offensive. Then we will survey the various components of the Muslim world audience along an ideological spectrum, and the reasons for crafting delivery messages for them. Despite the importance of geographical, cultural and linguistic differences among the world's ummah of between 800 million and a billion or more people, our immediate focus is more on adherents to particular ideologies rather than on national or ethnic lines. Islamist extremism is no longer unique to any culture or region, given its infiltration of countries with little or no Islamic tradition. Thus the battle within Islam is taking place in almost any country where there are Muslims, including what is traditionally known as the West. The ummah is now global.

Though discussing the ummah, we should keep in mind at all times that there is much more to today's ideological conflicts than extreme Islamism. Message strategies could pertain to traditional allies such as the United Kingdom, Australia, the Americas, Europe, South Korea, Southeast Asia and Japan; and countries with which we have complicated relationships such as India, Russia and China; and hotspots like Africa.

Finally, we will articulate the variegated messages, starting with the attack on the enemy, which is negative, and concluding with the positive, hopeful messages.

The virtues of the negative campaign

An approach to separate extremists from their popular support bases is unlikely to work if the terrorist fringe has greater credibility in the public eye than either the United States or "moderate" indigenous authorities. People seething with anger, resentment, disillusionment, humiliation, fear and other negative motivators are not normally receptive to warm messages from a power they view as an adversary, an enemy, or simply hypocritical or unjust.

Suspicious or even hostile people can open up if they can be persuaded that the power they perceive as unjust or misguided will protect them or their interests or at least treat them with respect. While for the moment it is difficult or impossible for many people abroad to be too closely identified with the United States, it is not difficult for them to be against America's enemies. We thus promote positive change as the product of a double negative: if we cannot be accepted as a friend through positive means, we can at least share a common cause by being an enemy of others' enemies. Though not an ideal relationship, it is far better than the status quo, so we should pocket it as progress. It is a kind of reasoning that many in the target areas understand.

This first task is an opportunity to deny the critics, as well as the enemy (and it is vital to differentiate between the two, though they might feed off one another for political gain) the ability to define or dominate the terms of debate and frames of reference. With a mutual agreement about the horrific nature of the enemy and the urgency with which the extremists must be defeated, the U.S. shares a common enemy with all of humanity. Thus, "the enemy of my enemy is my friend." Accentuation of the negative is logically the more important emphasis: it is easier, cheaper, faster and more powerful. Quicker results will shorten the war, reduce the pace of terrorist replenishment, encourage those not currently engaged, and save lives.

When negative is positive

In human nature, as we have seen, negative sentiments and themes tend to trump the positive, which helps explain why some of the most successful or powerful politicians, even if personally amicable or ethical, tend to run negative political campaigns. Human nature also illustrates how otherwise decent people will, by intimidation, inaction or even support, lose out to demagogues in power struggles, and how small bands of militants can control or dominate.

Some will argue that only demagogues and totalitarians act with negative attacks on their opponents. They are wrong. Political warfare has a strong place in American political tradition. Samuel Adams, the man Thomas Jefferson credited with shepherding the American Revolution, pioneered modern ideological warfare.

Adams mounted a negative ideological attack followed by a positive alternative solution, soundly based in easy-to-understand philosophical and moral terms. He combined intimidation with ideas. "It is a good Maxim in Politicks as well as in War to put & keep the Enemy in the Wrong," Adams counseled in 1775, always following his fearsome political attacks with a way out for the adversary and a positive, unifying vision for all.[129]

In much of today's Arab and Islamic cultures, as with mankind as a whole, the prevailing drivers are strongly negative. Hostilities and suspicions can last centuries, which is why words like "crusade" are so volatile even after hundreds of years. Negative campaigning energizes by appealing to the target audience's frustrations and fears. Negative campaigning mobilizes by initiative, leverage and momentum. Negative campaigning can provide satisfaction, relief, even optimism. Negative campaigning cuts through the rhetoric, logic, predispositions and prejudices of target audiences, and even plays to their strengths; it establishes basic issues and principles that separate friend from intractable foe. It can generate enormous peer pressure for positive ends. It can force people to take sides. Properly moderated or checked, negative campaigning creates the basic common ground that most of humanity ultimately shares and wishes to defend; and it awakens the complacent and drives them to become more involved and hopeful.

The long-term strategic goal of U.S. message-making must be to help restore the international prestige of the United States of America around the world, and win the "war of ideas" worldwide: not only among Arabs and Muslims, but among countries that traditionally have been close friends and allies.

A conventional approach to a strategy of variegated negative messages has the following objectives:

Support and strengthen our friends. U.S. messages must support friendly foreign governments, friendly opposition forces where the governments have not been cooperative, and friendly minority and exile groups from denied areas. They must also support the ambivalent to help them become supporters.

---

[129] For an excellent account of Samuel Adams' career as a political warrior and propagandist, see John K. Alexander, *Samuel Adams: America's Revolutionary Politician* (Rowman & Littlefield, 2002).

Win over the ambivalent. After demonstrating a common threat and a common enemy, unity against that enemy is vital. The U.S. must define the common enemy. The U.S. is the natural ally. Others do not have to like the U.S. or believe in it; but they should be persuaded to accept that we are the enemies of their enemies. From there we will find common ground on which we can build. Many know this but do not believe it. Others believe it but have no intellectual or political cover to allow them to know or express it. Still more are open to believing it, and beyond them, others are not closed to being persuaded. Not a few even think the United States is unserious or incapable of protecting them or defeating their enemies. Some fear betrayal and abandonment, for understandable reasons.

Divide the opposition to the United States and its allies. Opposition to the United States is broad and deep, but also deeply divided, and facing no serious sustained American political or psychological challenge. With a reasonable effort, the U.S. can divide its international opposition, both within the Islamic world and in established democracies. The U.S. can peel some outer layers from the terrorist-sympathizer camp, persuade others to cooperate or at least mute their criticism, and to focus their wrath on the common enemy (especially where the opposition is about American policies, and not fundamentally about the United States itself).

Disrupt, divide and destroy the terrorist networks and their support networks. As the military and intelligence services destroy enemy cadre and infrastructure, a strategic communication offensive must simultaneously attack the will of the enemy and its support base, encouraging suspicions, divisions, desertions, defections and fratricide. The offensive must allow certain of the terrorist cadre a means of escape, giving confidence that if they turn themselves in and collaborate with the U.S. and its allies, they will be able to live and have a hopeful and dignified future both from a secular perspective and within their cultural worldview.

The fatal flaw in this approach is its defensiveness. The approach dates from a time when we had fewer enemies and the world was an easier place to navigate. Our strategy must be to take and maintain the initiative. Today we need an accelerant, if only as a frame of reference that underscores the urgency of the situation. To illustrate, we take the conventional approach and flip it:

- Disrupt, divide and destroy the terrorist networks and their support networks;
- Divide the opposition to the United States and its allies;
- Win over the ambivalent; and
- Support and strengthen our friends.

As a result of these accelerating measures, the approach is no longer defensive and reactive because it presumes that we are already supporting and strengthening our friends. The new inverted approach, emphasizing a message attack on the enemy, takes the offensive alongside the military's counterinsurgency and counter-terrorism efforts. Rather than allow the enemy set the agenda in a new strategy of reacting to its propaganda attacks, we turn the tables around. We don't try to show how nice we are, but how evil and dangerous the enemy is, and in culturally appropriate contexts. That is the immediate-term objective of the variegated messages: to induce the enemy to destroy itself from within, and to destroy the enemy's credibility, his image and ideas in the eyes of his sympathizers and the rest of the world. The message must define the enemy, narrowly, to have no redeeming qualities, showing that it must be vanquished.[130]

The spectrum of the ummah

American politicians have defined the enemy already, but they have done so in a way better suited to rallying friends domestically and in other western democracies, rather than rallying enemies of the enemy. Extreme Islamists aim their ideological propaganda principally at the ummah in almost any corner of the world as part of the "battle within Islam." The radical Islamists wage propaganda warfare against the rest of the world as well, but mainly in support of their offensive within the ummah and for recruiting new converts.[131] Several approaches to combating the problem are being

---

[130] Demonization of the enemy is a sound doctrine, though any message strategy must take pains not to create a "Versailles effect" that would humiliate an entire nationality or culture and prevent a peaceful long-term outcome.

[131] One of the ways in which the extremists wage propaganda and political warfare within the United States is through civil rights networks that exaggerate incidence of "islamophobia" and demand special protections

debated at present, and some are under implementation. However, sharp divisions exist among highly informed and experienced experts about the optimal route.

In an important strategy paper titled *Civil Democratic Islam*, Cheryl Benard of the Rand Corporation sees four broad "positions" along a continuum in the Islamic world and offers approaches toward each, emphasizing relations with secular and "moderate" Muslims.[132] Antony Sullivan, from a quite different perspective, offers a plan for political and organizational collaboration with more traditional Muslims, including those he calls "moderate Islamists."[133] As with a spectrum of light, precise boundaries between positions are indistinct, but Benard's model of four Islamic positions – fundamentalists, traditionalists, modernists and secularists – and Sullivan's nuanced approach to language and traditional values are useful for designing a "spectrum of messages" in American public diplomacy and political warfare. Where this author departs from Benard's approach is his view that we should find allies among people whom many Westerners would not consider democratic or progressive. For our purposes, we should be content to work with those in the ummah who do not use violence and subversion against us. Reasonable people will disagree about exact distinctions, but Benard offers a good model as a point of departure.

Fundamentalists, in Benard's definition, "put forth an aggressive, expansionist version of Islam that does not shy away from violence.

---

and privileges. These operations are often aimed at intimidating critics, discouraging scrutiny, and obstructing criminal or intelligence investigations. By fanning fears of "islamophobia," practitioners reinforce senses of persecution and paranoia, and harden tendencies toward extremism. This, in turn, reinforces society's tendencies to pander to the militant voices and undermine the integrity of counterterrorism and security strategies.

[132] Cheryl Benard, *Civil Democratic Islam: Partners, Resources and Strategies* (RAND Corporation, 2003).

[133] Sullivan sees "moderate Islamists" as being committed to democratic governance and as sharing cultural concerns held by mainstream American conservatives, thus opening an area of mutual respect and understanding that can lead to collaboration. See Antony T. Sullivan, "Conservative Ecumenism: Politically Incorrect Meditations on Islam and the West," delivered at The Historical Society's conference on "Reflections on the Current State of Historical Inquiry," Boothbay Harbor, Maine, June 4, 2004.

They want to gain political power and then impose strict public observance of Islam, as they themselves define it, forcibly on as broad a population worldwide as possible." They seek political power in individual countries as steps toward a worldwide Islamic political movement and ultimately a reestablished caliphate. They form, therefore, a political movement.

However, Benard draws distinctions within the fundamentalist position: the *scriptural fundamentalists*, rooted in a religious establishment such as Shi'ites and Wahhabis and adherents to defined theology; and *radical fundamentalists*, which are "much less concerned with the literal substance of Islam, with which they take considerable liberties either deliberately or because of ignorance of orthodox Islamic doctrine." Al Qaeda and the Taliban belong to the radical fundamentalist group. Though "not all fundamentalists embrace or even endorse terrorism, at least not the indiscriminate type of terrorism that targets civilians and often kills Muslims along with the 'enemy,'" Benard writes, fundamentalists as a whole embrace a civilization that is incompatible with Western values.[134]

Even so, traditionalists and fundamentalists are important allies in places like Afghanistan, and once we win the support of traditional leaders, we are most likely to win the support of their people. Messages and policies that promote alien Western lifestyle and political norms threaten such allies.

Fundamentalists must no longer be dismissed as fringe elements. Their ideologies are serious and deserve serious treatment. Their differences with the West have less to do with government policies or diplomatic conflicts and more with theological and lifestyle issues, and they leave little room for discussion, in Benard's view. There are important exceptions. The U.S. should be sending messages constantly to both groups of fundamentalists. (This presents us with the problem of Saudi Arabia, an "ally" that is the single most powerful sponsor of the enemy ideology that spawns most of the terrorism around the world.)

Traditionalists are desirous of a conservative Muslim society and tend to be suspicious of modernity and innovation. Benard places them in two significantly different types: *conservative traditionalists* and *reformist traditionalists*. Traditionalists are generally moderate and adapt to their political and social environments. They have widespread social, political and moral legitimacy; they are usually

---

[134] Benard, pp. 3-4.

tolerant and respectful of other religions; they represent a much broader swath of Islamic society than the fundamentalists do; they are organized and institutionalized, and in many places they represent the social mainstream.

The conservative traditionalists seek to follow Islamic law and tradition "rigorously and literally," with the state serving as a facilitator as circumstances permit. Conservative traditionalist Muslims "do not generally favor violence and terrorism," through many traditionalists aid and abet terrorists with resources, shelter, intelligence and other forms of support. Modern life and the temptations that come with it are a threat. The prospect of change meets fear and, understandably, resistance. Reformist traditionalists are seen as less literal in the application of their religion, and more open to social reforms, though they tend to be cautious in adapting to social change.[135] Sullivan writes of a *"moderate* Islamist movement" devoted to democratic governance, economic development and so forth, "anchored in traditional cultural values" and sharing interests with American cultural conservatives, especially on matters of family, morality and lifestyle.[136] The distinction is important, as it challenges the stereotypes that all Islamists are violent or otherwise hostile or extreme.

Modernists, in Benard's model, believe in eternal Islamic truths but see historical and cultural circumstances as governing the ways in which those truths are lived and observed. Consequently they seek to change the present "orthodox understanding and practice of Islam," identifying an "essential core" of the faith that can be strengthened instead of weakened by change. "Their core values – the primacy of the individual conscience and a community based on social responsibility, equality, and freedom – are easily compatible with modern democratic norms." In Benard's words, "the modernist vision matches our own."[137]

However, in many Muslim countries and regions the modernists are at a terrible disadvantage. They lack well-established power bases that would provide them with taxes or regular charitable contributions, independent income from businesses and foundations, and "captive audiences" through mosques, schools, social programs

---

[135] Benard, pp. 4-5.
[136] Sullivan, "Conservative Ecumenism: Politically Incorrect Meditations on Islam and the West," op. cit.
[137] Benard, pp. 5, 37.

and modern media. In many places, including countries like Egypt and Pakistan, the modernists are in physical danger of being accused of apostasy and other Islamic crimes, can be denied the right to write or work, and given harsh judicial sentences.[138] They are also vulnerable to physical attack from fundamentalist extremists with few to protect them.

Secularists, the last of the four positions in Benard's model, draw a sharp distinction between one's personal spiritual values and government. In their belief, the state must not interfere with an individual's exercise of religious faith. Secularists range from totalitarian Ba'athists on one extreme to libertarians, socialists and nihilists who believe that individuals' faith and religious customs are personal private matters and that government must be divorced completely from God.

Benard devotes considerable attention to the traits of fundamentalists, traditionalists, modernists and secularists, providing clues about how to distinguish one from another, and offering a table of "marker issues" to illustrate major ideological positions within Islam. She identifies potentially useful democratic factors as well as dangers for U.S. policymakers. A selection of marker issues offers examples of how one might benefit from differences among each of the positions and craft messages with the most impact.[139]

First, however, is the question of the strategic approach. In her thesis of promoting "positive change" in the form of democracy, modernity, and compatibility in Islamic parts of the world, Benard argues that "the United States and the West need to consider very carefully which elements, trends, and forces within Islam they intend to strengthen; what the goals and values of their various potential allies and protégés really are; and what the broader consequences of advancing their respective agendas are likely to be." She calls for

---

[138] Benard, p. 39.

[139] In her monograph, Benard offers a two-page table of "'Marker Issues' and the Major Ideological Positions in Islam." On the X axis, she identifies radical fundamentalists, scriptural fundamentalists, conservative traditionalists, reformist traditionalists, modernists, mainstream secularists, and radical secularists. On the Y axis she lists the marker issues: democracy, human rights and individual liberties, polygamy, and Islamic criminal penalties. See Benard, pp. 8-9.

supporting the modernists first, helping the traditionalists against the fundamentalists, and confronting and opposing the latter.[140]

Benard and her colleagues elaborate further in a follow-on study titled *Building Moderate Muslim Networks*, which calls for borrowing from the successful strategies of the Cold War.[141] At the same time, in places like Afghanistan, traditionalists and even fundamentalists are important allies against our common enemy. What follows is a suggestion of how to negate that unpleasant situation in the near-term, with an eye toward reversing it over time.

Isolating the terrorists from their bases of support

As indicated in Chapter 1, the terrorist social environment can be illustrated as a set of concentric spheres similar to the layers of an onion. For the purposes of simplicity, we will use a two-dimensional model of concentric rings to illustrate the social support structure and the opportunities that structure affords us. This basic model allows for many ideological, cultural, tribal, clan, organizational and factional differences and is merely intended as a general conceptual guide.

The most intractable terrorists are located at the rotten core. These are the leaders. They include "combatants," command and control, and ideological leaders, including the overt radicalized clerics and Islamic centers. The fully-corrupted hard core is the most intractable part of the enemy and must be dealt with in the harshest of terms. Immediately surrounding that core are the terrorist followers, the lower-level or newer "combatants" and ideologues. They are followers in that they were recruited, indoctrinated, brainwashed or otherwise inspired into joining the terrorist force. Many are graduates of Saudi-funded extremist madrassas or al Qaeda training camps, or veterans of wars in the former Yugoslavia, Chechnya, Afghanistan and Iraq. They, too, are the equivalent of military targets but some of their members might be converted away from deadly extremism in ways that would be politically or psychologically useful for the counterterrorism cause.

The next circle consists of the hard operational support network. This is a network of individuals and organizations, including

---

[140] Benard, pp. x-xi.

[141] Angel Rabasa, Cheryl Benard, Lowell H. Schwartz and Peter Sickle, *Building Moderate Muslim Networks* (RAND Corporation, 2007).

religious institutions and charities that are conscious and committed facilitators of terrorist violence or extremism. This network provides logistical support, shelter, communications, denial and deception capabilities, financial support, humanitarian aid for families, first aid, propaganda, and legal assistance.

Surrounding the hard operational support network is a network of looser operational support. These include individuals and organizations who support the terrorist cause in a less active, more passive fashion, but who are nevertheless committed to the cause. Ideological control is not as rigid as in the inner circles, and is therefore easier to fracture.

Moving further outward is a circle that includes the more reluctant or timid supporters. They may not be as ideologically indoctrinated or committed, but they support the terrorists out of tribal, linguistic, religious, social or cultural loyalties. Many will support the extremists out of intimidation or fear. Others do because their leaders implicitly or explicitly wish it. Some express their support merely by looking the other way or staying out of trouble. Others might be "all talk and no action," meaning that they might support or sympathize with the terrorists out of genuine enthusiasm, but they lack real courage or fanaticism and can easily betray their friends. This circle is relatively easy to penetrate.

Around the circle of reluctant supporters is a ring of the ambivalent – those who do not wish to be part of the movement but who are reluctant to cooperate with the authorities either. They may be passive supporters, passive neutrals, or even passive opponents. Their passivity or ambivalence, however, makes them a hindrance to counterterrorism or counterinsurgency efforts and therefore an asset of the adversary. In the outermost circle encircling the ambivalent are everybody else, the majority of Muslims (in general) who oppose the extremists and are open to taking part in activity against them but are not actively doing so. These concentric circles exist in Western countries in addition to traditionally Muslim states.

Attack sequence 1:
Break the cohesion and spirit of the extremists

Breaking the cohesion and spirit of the extremists requires detailed intelligence and cultural insights about the targets. The idea is to create and deliver messages that undermine the image of the enemy leadership in each layer or ring of the metaphoric onion.

The messages should create, reopen or exacerbate internal differences, cause the leadership to overreact, quarrel, or otherwise lose control; and encourage desertions, defections, denunciations and fratricide within the enemy camp. The messages should rapidly produce opportunities to exploit for intelligence and psychological warfare/information operations purposes, and for public diplomacy purposes.

Every possible case of infighting, denunciation or desertion needs publicity. Every overt defector is an opportunity to expose the enemy's inner nature, as well as a means to damage extremist morale and encourage further splits, desertions and defections.[142] Intelligence services should record the bickering and odd personal traits of enemy leaders, especially those who inspire personal or ideological loyalties, for release to the public on television, radio, the Internet and DVDs to tear away the aura of decisive or moral leadership.

This requires agility and imagination that bureaucracies discourage, and speed that challenges the nation's top-heavy decision-making process. It requires an almost numbing relentlessness of constant repetition and amplification. As with military combat operations, the ways of public diplomacy and public affairs must adapt to fight the war of ideas like a real war.

Every attempt by other extremists to distance themselves from the main target likewise requires magnification and publicity to show how indeed isolated the terrorist core has become. Intra-extremist rivalries must be exploited for their political and psychological value. Message-makers must suppress the temptation to validate the splittist extremists or think of them as trustworthy or reformed.

Likewise, message-makers must be prepared to defend against criticism that they are promoting messages of anti-western clerics. They must be confidently convinced that amplifying the denunciations of extremists by other hard-liners works in the U.S. interest to isolate the hard core in the near-term, yet without weakening the more moderate voices over the long term. Anathematization of the extremists by recognized religious authorities in the form of fatwas or other statements, even and perhaps especially by those deemed more "conservative" and anti-

---

[142] Some extremists might defect to non-Muslims in hope of leniency. Others would prefer handing themselves over to fellow Muslims. Either way, message policies must be in place to exploit defector opportunities.

Western, provides the credible condemnation needed. We need only show the extremists' own isolation in what they perceive to be their camp.

Attack sequence 2: Split away the outward rings

A second message goal is to free many Muslims of one of their perceived adversaries and foster a sense of urgency in the rest of the world. The action must produce open expressions of shame and revulsion in the community in which the terrorists operate, and embolden anti-extremist resisters. The powerful, negative messages must accurately portray the extremist enemy as an enemy of Islam and therefore of humanity, and one handled most properly by Islamic authorites themselves. Again, recapturing the language is vital. Shame and revulsion should mobilize Muslim leaders against the extremists as part of protecting their own moral legitimacy and the public honor of the ummah (in part denouncing, as the Spanish Muslims did, the Islamist extremists as apostates and therefore not Muslim). The messages must prompt or help Muslims to craft and direct their own messages to redeem the public honor of all believers in Muhammad's teachings.[143]

---

[143] The U.S. did not do that after 9/11. Even as the president personally reached out to Muslim leaders in the U.S. and repeatedly cautioned the public that Islam was not the enemy, most American Muslim leaders showed a greater fixation with perceived discrimination and undue FBI surveillance against them than with helping root terrorist elements from their community and aid the war effort. Several leaders' delicate balancing acts on terrorism caused divisions in the community. The American Muslim Council, the principal umbrella group, disbanded after its executive director declined on at least three occasions to denounce al Qaeda by name in public. Two of the movement's main leaders, Sami Al-Arian and AMC founder Abrurahman Alamoudi, were convicted of terrorism-related crimes and sentenced to federal prison, as were several leaders or former leaders of the Council on American-Islamic Relations (CAIR). Their persistent, shrill campaign damaged law enforcement's counterterrorism activities and gave the distinct impression to much of the American public that American Muslims were not against terrorism at all, but were indeed subversive and dangerous forces to be distrusted and fought. This was extremely unfortunate, as the situation gravely damaged the image of American Muslims. The Spanish fatwa against bin Laden and terrorism, issued on the anniversary of the Madrid transit bombings, specifically noted how the extremism and failure to fight the terrorists fueled what it called

Attack sequence 3: Reinforce the "enemy of their enemy"

The primary order here is to defeat the notion that the United States is at war with Islam. This is the most crucial strategic message of all: to show credibility. Part of credibility is that the messenger understands and believes the message he is delivering – that the U.S. is an ally. The "we are not at war with Islam" mantra is a loser issue. It is a weak, defensive response to an allegation that many people, Muslim and non-Muslim, already believe. It fails to refute the allegation being raised. It merely protests that "we're not out to kill all of you." That is no message; it generates little credibility or confidence, and therefore no trust or even understanding. It is the same unfortunate type of message that U.S. propagandists directed at the Japanese toward the end of World War II. In a bid to persuade them to quit the fight, the Allies told the Japanese that if they surrendered we would not exterminate them. That message, and fear that the Allies would capture or kill the Emperor, inspired greater resistance.[144]

An alternative message shows that the world is under attack by those who warp Islam to suit their violent, sociopathic ideologies and visions, and that the U.S. has been allied with Muslims around the world as Muslim people reclaim the very faith and culture that the extremists are trying to steal from them. Muslims are our natural allies against the extremists, and it is absurd for some to claim that we are at war with our allies.

Such a message will fall on hard ground unless we can re-direct many Muslims' concept of their sworn enemy. By saying we are not fighting Islam as we bomb "bad" Muslims, and despite all efforts to avoid collateral damage we still harm and kill innocent men, women and children. We make ourselves look like liars as well as mortal enemies. By demonstrating that the U.S. is helping Muslim people take back their mosques from terrorists and their countries from tyrants and fanatics, and by citing Islamic leaders who authoritatively declare the fanatics to be anti-Muslim, we are

---

"islamophobia." American Muslim leaders issued no such comprehensive fatwa.

[144] For more on counterproductive propaganda that unintentionally strengthens the enemy's will to keep fighting, see Herbert Romerstein, "Counterpropaganda," in *Strategic Influence*, op. cit.

illustrating a common cause. American leaders have offered this message almost constantly since 9/11, not least at the presidential level, but have been handicapped by the lack of credibility of the messengers with their respective audiences, timid follow-through in the government bureaucracy, poor coordination with the private sector, and an overall incoherent strategic approach. This means that civil Muslims must ultimately take on the largest and most important state sponsors of warped terrorist ideologies. The proper U.S. role should be to amplify and repeat the messages rather than overtly originate them.

U.S. policy, and therefore the message, should seek to cleave and widen as many divisions as possible among the opposition. It must do as little as possible to enable extremist factions to reunite, create and support as many nodes of counter-opposition as possible. It must stimulate, support and unite nodes of support among friends and allies. At this point, we approach the message-making not by "position" within Islam, but by issues and ideas.

Crucial to this effort is taking back the language and using the proper cultural terms, while abandoning use of the definitions that the extremists created to change the frame of reference. We addressed the importance of words in Chapters 2 and 3.

Instead of promoting liberal change and a positive American image as a starting point, the emphasis should be to halt the enemy's momentum first, strip the enemy of its traditionalist support base, expose and exploit the enemy's vulnerabilities and inner divisions, and destroy the enemy's image and credibility while helping the positive changes to follow.[145]

Follow-on messages: Support and partnership

If the primary messages demonize the enemy and seek to induce the taking of sides by negative means, the secondary or follow-on messages are designed to turn mutual opposition to the enemy into

---

[145] At this point, we are faced with the question of whom to support. This is best addressed on a case-by-case basis. Do we want to alienate and perhaps radicalize the traditionalists by suddenly challenging their way of life by aggressively promoting modernism and secularism? Do we want to impose democracy or big central government on traditional societies based on clans and sheikhs, thus giving them cause to oppose us? Or do we simply leave everybody alone once the extremists are eliminated, so the people can deal with their own differences among themselves, without outside interference?

understanding and tolerance of the United States and its allies, and ultimately open support and partnership.

These are positive messages. They are secondary in short-term importance for the practical reason that positive messages tend to produce results more slowly and require near-constant maintenance and reinforcement than negative messages – much like the "three-block war" concept in which peacekeeping and humanitarian relief operations occur within three contiguous city blocks of combat forces.[146] Many of the secondary messages, and the means of delivering them, are similar to what is generally considered public diplomacy, and indeed this is the point where traditional public diplomacy becomes operational. Secondary messages are vital and may be deployed simultaneously alongside, or immediately following, the primary messages. They are called secondary messages because of the order in which they are to be deployed for near-term results in the war of ideas.

This dividing line of primary versus secondary messages shows how public diplomacy, as conventionally understood, is insufficient and in some ways subordinate in fighting idea battles. The accelerant of hard, often harsh, and almost always negative messages is incompatible with public diplomacy as traditionally practiced. The task requires a separate agency with a combat or national security function and culture. By keeping public diplomacy separate from the accelerant, we maintain the public diplomacy instrument's positive nature and integrity, while insulating the accelerant from the softer side of strategic communication. Since this report is devoted to the content and nature of messages, it is not the place to discuss the modalities.

Spectrum of messages

As in electoral politics, for the message to be credible with the intended audience, it must be tailored to each particular "constituency." The message must always be truthful. To complicate factors, the messages must always be consistent with one another, never contradictory. In the case of the war effort, the constituencies fall in three broad categories: the terrorists and their supporters and sympathizers; the United States, its traditional friends and allies,

---

[146] Gen. Charles C. Krulak, "Cultivating Intuitive Decisionmaking," *Marine Corps Gazette*, May, 1999.

including in traditionally Muslim societies, and the friendlies in contested areas; and the rest of the world. These categories do not pit the U.S. against the ummah; they winnow the terrorist camp into the first category, maintain much of the Islamic world in the traditional friends-and-allies camp, and recognize the many Muslims among others who are neither friend nor foe.

Islam is only a part of the war of ideas. Part of the hard adversary camp includes non-Muslims intractably hostile to the United States and its allies. They include the regimes in North Korea, Cuba and Venezuela and their international followers, as well as activist and militant non-governmental organizations and networks inside the United States, the United Kingdom, and across Europe and elsewhere. Again, a cautionary note: among the opposition, the genuine enemy often travels in the same currents as the legitimate dissenter and the two must never be confused.[147] The spectrum, then, is stratified not along geographical or cultural lines, but along the lines of transnational ideas and ideologies.

The second category includes not only traditional friends and allies that fully support the U.S., but others who are working with the United States in the war effort as overt or secret members of the coalitions of the willing, and those who oppose U.S. policy but remain in the general community of American friends and allies (i.e., in Latin America). Many Muslim countries, or countries with large Muslim populations, are among the United States' traditional friends and allies (the new government in Iraq is also in the second category), and it is as much in their interests to be working with the United States against the terrorists as it is for the U.S. itself. In this category, U.S. themes should be aimed at helping build and fortify domestic support for the war effort in each respective country, both to make it easier for the national leaders to continue their support (in which there could be bilateral collaborative information/action relationship) and to make it difficult for others to continue their opposition.

---

[147] The enemy will attempt to manipulate or otherwise influence the honest dissenter or loyal opposition, requiring on the message-maker's part rigorous counterintelligence safeguards to ensure that terrorist entities' influence is monitored, minimized, and ultimately eliminated. For its part, the loyal opposition must face this reality with open eyes and diligently work to keep agents of foreign powers or causes from exploiting them. Where it fails to do so, we must challenge it to take sides and provide necessary support.

The third category, the "rest of the world," is lower in *immediate* priority but still extremely important. The U.S. must address the often strong opposition there. Some countries and regimes are secretly cooperating with the United States, but remain publicly potentially adversarial for other reasons. In the cases of Russia and China, that opposition predates 9/11 and is unrelated to the extreme Islamist issue; the excessive focus on radical Islamism at the expense of Russia, China and other places is a grave strategic error, and the cannibalizing of message-making capabilities to those regions to free up funds for short-term needs in focused areas is an indication of the lack of warfighting approach that characterizes the State Department and other parts of government.

Messengers

Though often not a credible messenger for the negative accelerant in Islamic societies on religious or cultural issues, the U.S. can still light the prairie fires. Repeated official public pronouncements and broadcasts of those who do have credibility are two easy and cost-free ways to start and fuel the new dialogue. The U.S. has the overt public diplomacy and traditional diplomatic means, the military information and psychological means, and the covert operational means – civilian and military – to force others to confront, address and discuss the issues. In the positive messages, the United States should normally (but not always) receive the credit along with its allies who would benefit; it must also never appear isolated in its negativity.

Messages directed at the terrorist core

Well-chosen primary messages will get into the heads of the terrorists and would-be terrorists themselves. None in the terrorist core are likely to entertain reasoned arguments coming from Washington or those deemed its surrogates. None would be expected to respond positively to overtly American messages, especially on matters of ideology. But the terrorist core is still vulnerable to well-delivered messages.

Terrorist supporters and recruits will have a strong ideological and material structure of mutual support, as we saw in the concentric circle metaphor. Around the ideological and material support structure is a social environment that affirms the extremists' mission and esteems their sacrifice, providing crucial psychological support as well as safe haven that remove or overwhelm the terrorists' lingering doubts or qualms, or provide the necessary reinforcement and reassurance that repress each terrorist's personal fears or feed his fanaticism or courage.[148] These structures often insulate the terrorist from information or ideas that would conflict with, and therefore undermine, the strict ideological indoctrination, peer pressure, and the sincerely-held hopes for eternal supernatural rewards that motivate and strengthen him. Many of the structures are housed in mosques and Islamic centers that have sponsored overt or covert extremist preaching.

A complicating factor in this is a tendency for a community perceiving itself to be under ideological attack (or even simple criticism) to unite against critics and law-enforcement. The defensive community will become overly defensive to the point of protecting the extremists among them from outsiders. This reflex creates an outward impression or inward atmosphere – and a reality – of sympathy or collaboration. It creates a vicious circle of suspicion and counter-suspicion that leads to a persecution complex, marginalization, and deepened hostility.

We understand that the belief in pleasing God and trusting in an afterlife of carnal pleasure are foremost in most of the extremists' minds as they kill, and even in their last living seconds as they greet their impending death. The slogans (*Allahu akhbar*, God is great), chanted in the cockpit by the United Airlines Flight 93 hijackers as they flew the jetliner into the Pennsylvania field on 9/11, as well as by the most professionally trained and battle-hardened insurgents in Iraq as U.S. Marines pick them off one by one, testify to the terrorists' deep ideological conviction. The suicide bomber who plowed his vehicle into a crowd of children in a Baghdad street in July 2005 shouted "Allahu akhbar" as he detonated his bomb.

Attack the core ideological beliefs

Where we cannot kill such elements before they attack, we should strive to shake the fanatics' confidence in their cause and their rewards by directly and relentlessly attacking their core ideological

---

[148] This does not include, obviously, situations where the individual is isolated and drugged prior to being deployed against his will as a human bomb.

beliefs. It may not be necessary to persuade them of the *wrongness* of their cause; one need only plant enough doubt in their minds about the *rightness* of it and about what might happen to their families and their souls after they detonate their suicide bombs. Thanks to forceful and principled statements from a few Muslim leaders, one can reach into their minds without necessarily knowing who or where they are. A 2005 fatwa issued by 170 Muslim scholars in Amman, according to an American Muslim interfaith advisor to King Abdullah of Jordan, was intended to "put doubt in the minds" of terrorists who trust the exhortations of extremist clerics. Would-be terrorists, he said, must be made to know that their spiritual leaders' guidance is against Islamic law.[149]

Muslim leaders have issued plentiful authoritative fatwas and powerful sermons, though few in English, making U.S. collection and redistribution difficult.[150] The fatwas are important weapons against extremism. It took nearly four years for American Muslim leaders to issue a formal fatwa against terrorism – a delay that only deepened suspicions of them – but they did so in August, 2005. That declaration, and an even more powerful one issued by Spanish Muslims, shared common themes that frame the most basic message to sow doubt among the extremists:

- The extremists are to blame for discrediting the name of Islam and blackening the face of the Prophet;
- The extremists are to blame for the Muslim people's fears in Western societies, discrimination, lack of acceptance, lack of trust, "Islamophobia," etc.; and
- The extremists are to blame for the Muslim people's hardships in traditional Islamic lands.

---

[149] Sana Abdullah, "Muslim scholars 'forbid' labeling apostasy," UPI, July 6, 2005. "The Islamic conference's final statement made no political references and did not condemn terrorism against civilians," UPI reported. It was another black eye against Muslims. The following day, when the wire story appeared in the newspapers saying that the Jordan group failed to condemn terrorism against civilians, Islamist terrorists bombed the London subway transit system.

[150] The U.S. and British governments have expansive resources for making immediate translations, but a senior official tells the author that the office of the Under Secretary of State for Public Diplomacy did not view most of the documents as important enough to translate.

Attack, divide, sow doubt, peel away support

Meanwhile, general policy should be: (1) to send messages that drive as many divisions as possible among the opposition, (2) to permit as few opportunities as possible to unite it; (3) to aid, create, facilitate and amplify as many nodes of counter-opposition as possible, and (4) to fortify friends and allies.

Divided they fall

Exacerbation of divisions has several tangible effects for the war effort. It undermines the enemy's unity of command. The U.S. was surprised to see radical Sunnis and Shi'ites collaborating with one another and with marginalized Ba'athists in Iraq. While they fought one another, the foreign presence unified them in certain ways, even as Iraq appears headed toward civil war. The U.S. and its allies should be using information and messages to split enemy factions into factions that turn against one another instead of the coalition, the Iraqi government, or civil society. Tactical information operations should be integrated across services, agencies and alliances constantly to exacerbate internal stresses and friction in the enemy camp.

Radicals in Indonesia and Egypt should know of the constant infighting and fratricide in Iraq. The Coalition can play upon characteristics of conspiratorial organizations in a high state of alert within a traditionally conspiratorially-minded culture to cause extremist leaders to lose trust in one another and to suspect one another of disloyalty, or even of secretly collaborating with the authorities or "infidels."

The Coalition can play on these fears with opportunity-driven messages. Stresses and fractures almost invariably produce valuable intelligence for the U.S. and its allies, through increased or indiscreet communications that can be intercepted, intra-factional arguments that spill into the open, and by desertions and defections. Some of this intelligence, properly handled, can be used not just for immediate and localized needs, but for public diplomacy and political warfare purposes. Presently such intelligence is considered mainly for surveillance, law enforcement, post-terrorism investigations and tactical combat support. Military lawyers and public affairs officers often prohibit the use of such intelligence for information operations – a practice that the combat leadership has tolerated even at the expense of the troops.

Internal divisions are a sign of lost confidence and weakness. Individuals in the adjacent concentric rings should begin to have second thoughts and act on them, diminishing the enemy's operational ability, further spreading the faultlines and providing more public diplomacy and political warfare opportunities. The main theme is that the extremists are harming Islam. It is crucial to sustain this theme by fortifying acceptable spokesmen courageous or confident enough to pronounce and repeat it; the U.S. should keep the pressure on, as a brother encouraging a brother, to maintain the message from credible figures, and to expand the numbers and stature of those repeating the themes. Part of the equation requires encouraging and, when necessary, challenging local leaders to stand up and defend their society and culture against the extremist attack, and to hold the pressure until they do.

Thus Muslims are defending their faith not from the Americans or outside the ummah where the religion is not under outside attack – Muslims worship more freely in the United States than anywhere else on Earth – but from the apostate hijackers within. The message must highlight the extreme teachings and interpretations, and shame others into repudiating by name the individuals responsible. This is a case where the president of the United States and other senior U.S. figures should shun naming any individual adversary (which has the unintended effect of uniting others around the enemy, as we saw in the chapter on branding), and leave it to respective political and cultural leaders themselves who already have done so. American strategic communicators can provide the necessary provocation and amplification.

Experience in the U.S. has shown that recalcitrant Muslim leaders will ultimately denounce – publicly and loudly – extremist ideology and extremist leaders *once that ideology and those leaders are isolated, highlighted, and held up for public scrutiny and opprobrium*. Many of the most outspoken American Muslim leaders have tended to react with excessive defensiveness, attacking the messenger and his motivation and not addressing the criticism. Usually the non-Muslim messenger, fearful of being labeled a bigot, will back down at the earliest allegation of prejudice or cultural insensitivity.

However, when the messenger remains firm without backing down to the near-inevitable accusations and politely maintains the offensive, the defensive leaders will be forced ultimately to confront the actual message itself and issue a value judgment on it. Some will try to avoid the issue by acting neutral or by obfuscating. Some will protest that they have already denounced terrorism and that further pressure on them is only to marginalize or humiliate them. Others, though, will try desperately to distance themselves from extremism, either tactically to hide their radicalism or, most frequently, strategically and sincerely because they reject the extremist ideology and fear being painted with the same brush.[151]

Tipping point

After the U.S. amplifies the voices of the Muslim leaders who denounce the extremists by name – and persuades its able allies, especially in predominantly Islamic societies, to do the same – the political dynamic should turn favorably. Latent fissures in the enemy camp open and widen. Almost nobody wants to be the first to raise his head; but others will join as momentum builds. The message maker must keep pushing for more and more leaders to issue their own denunciations, widening splits within the concentric circles immediately surrounding the extremists, and turning the radical elements against one another or isolating them completely. Such might have been the case when Abu Musab al-Zarqawi, the al Qaeda leader in Iraq, caused such revulsion by bombing a Muslim wedding party in Jordan that other al Qaeda leaders openly dressed him down. Jordanian intelligence and a captured al Qaeda member helped lead U.S. forces to kill Zarqawi in June, 2006.[152]

As these events unfold (again, usually with help), the public diplomat and strategic communicator must chronicle the

---

[151] This was the specific pattern after 9/11, especially in the cases of the leader of the North American cell of the Palestinian Islamic Jihad, Sami al-Arian, and Muslim Brotherhood and al Qaeda financier Abdurahman Alamoudi. Both are now in federal prison on terrorism-related convictions. The American Muslim Council (AMC), an umbrella group founded by Alamoudi that included many mainstream Islamic figures who strongly opposed extremism, fell apart after Alamoudi's exposure as a supporter of Hezbollah and his conviction on federal terrorism charges as part of a plot to assassinate the crown prince (now king) of Saudi Arabia, and after the AMC executive director refused repeatedly to denounce al Qaeda by name.

[152] Kim Gamel and Robert Burns, "U.S. Moves to Stop Zarqawi Network in Iraq," Associated Press, June 9, 2006.

denunciations: who is rejecting the ideology, what is a particular figure's moral authority or social standing, and whom the figure represents, along with places, dates, times and other circumstances. The denunciations quickly must be transcribed and compiled, with all supporting material, and distributed widely in many languages and media, along with as much new video and other imagery as possible. Part of the power of the message is frequent, often even daily increases in intensity against the adversary. In conjunction with constant exposés of radical rhetoric, doctrine, intentions, behavior, corruption, hypocrisy, perversions and atrocities, the isolation effort will attract more adherents as momentum builds against the evil-doing unbelievers, the mufsidoon and the kafir as we saw in Chapter 3.

Setting up the enemy to self-destruct

As terrorist violence continues and extremist Islamists inflict mass murder on other Muslims, the enemy might be setting itself up to self-destruct. The July 2005 slaying of Egypt's top diplomat in Iraq and the bombing of the resort town of Sharm el-Sheik uncorked Egyptian critics, even in the government-dominated media and among the government-appointed clerics, who openly vilified the Cairo regime for having tolerated, and at times encouraged, extremist ideology that fostered terrorist violence. "There is no use denying . . . . We incited the crime of Sharm el-Sheik," ran an editorial headline. The terrorists "didn't just conjure up in our midst suddenly, they are a product of a society that produces extremist fossilized minds that are easily controlled," said the editorial. "They became extremists through continuous incitement for extremism which we have allowed to exist in our societies. Regrettably, the incitement is coming from mosque pulpits, newspapers and TV screens, and radio microphones," all state-run. A columnist in the Egyptian newspaper *Al-Ahram* wrote, "This is not just deviation, it is a culture."[153]

Even fundamentalists are becoming more critical of the terrorists. Saudi Arabian Grand Mufti Sheikh Abdul Aziz al-Asheikh condemned those attempting to foment civil war in Iraq, placing

---

[153] Nadia Abou-el Magd, "Egyptians Question Culture-Extremism Link," Associated Press, July 27, 2005.

them in league with the 9/11 hijackers and pronouncing them as serving "the aims of the enemies conspiring against Muslims."[154] Saudi clerics are some of the less attractive sources for American message-making, but for the immediate term are among the most important, considering their credibility in their own fundamentalist and extremist communities, so their voices are important to amplify.[155]

Some American policymakers understandably will object to publicizing fundamentalist statements against the terrorists, as those same critics can be the most bitter sources of hostility and even violence toward the United States and its allies. The importance of lending them a voice is that they are trusted in the fundamentalist camps where "moderates" are not, and therefore are valuable immediate-term weapons to split the worst. Some of the voices support terrorist attacks on American military personnel and other American targets. Airing those voices will be difficult for some to accept. So was aligning with Stalin to defeat Hitler. Defeating the Soviets could wait, as long as the U.S. and its allies kept their eyes on the prize. Voices of former enemies are weapons that ultimately work in favor of the mission to split the enemy, isolate the most intransigent, and subdue the will to fight us.

Focus on the attackers

After establishing that Islam is under attack from within, and not without, the messages focus on the attackers themselves. The messages may be delivered as direct, accusatory charges against the inner core of the notional concentric rings to vilify and stigmatize in the eyes of other Muslims, while serving as an educational and inspirational message for others. The Zarqawi example after the

---

[154] "Saudi Cleric Condemns Iraqi Militants," UPI citing *Arab News*, September 20, 2005.
[155] The Saudis should be encouraged to expand their domestic deprogramming of extreme Islamists as aggressively as they have indoctrinated them around the world. They are reported to be successful to some degrees at rehabilitating Islamist radicals at home. Roula Khalaf, "Giving up jihad [sic] for an easy life in the Kingdom," *Financial Times*, April 2, 2007; and Roula Khalaf, "Saudis turn to Internet to thwart terror recruiting," *Financial Times*, April 2, 2007.

Jordan wedding attack is a case in point. Literally thousands of other cases remain to be individually chronicled and portrayed in vivid, highly visual forms.

Appeal to reason and self-interest

It is extremely difficult physically to penetrate the inner core of the extremist movement. But it is nevertheless possible to penetrate it by means of messages to get into the heads of individual terrorists before they complete their missions. In this case, the appeal should be to the individual terrorist's reason and self-interest; specifically, honor and the afterlife. An attacker who knows his action will bring him instant death believes he is giving his life to defend his people and bring them honor, sacrificing for his creator, and earning an eternity in paradise. He is acting rationally and therefore is using his sense of reason. *By killing himself or getting himself killed, he rationally believes he is acting in his own self-interests.*

Our job is to make him have second thoughts somewhere along the way from recruitment to pushing the detonator. He should be asking himself, "Am I really about to earn what my superiors promised? Am I really bringing honor to my family and people? Do I really believe what I believe?" The goal is to induce the target to question his cause and abort his mission, and to inspire others to do the same. Palestinian suicide bombers have turned themselves in on harboring such doubts.[156]

Family pride can be an important support mechanism for the terrorist who kills and dies. The belief that he is honoring his loved ones who appreciate his conviction and righteousness both motivates the fighter and provides an opportunity for us as message-makers. Some families are indeed proud of their terrorist children, but others are anguished, torn apart and even ostracized among their peers. As with anti-drunken driving advertisements, the messages must vividly

---

[156] This gets down to the question of what to do with the remains of terrorists, insurgents or other combatants not covered under the Geneva Conventions. U.S. policy in general is to return them when possible to families or clans, where they often receive a martyr's burial. There are other civilized ways to dispose of terrorist bodies while preventing both the type of burial culturally befitting a "martyr" and the creation of a gravesite shrine that could rally militant opposition to the U.S. and inspire new extremists. Those alternate civilized ways of disposing of terrorist bodies include cremation and burial at sea (or both).

show the pain of the terrorists' mothers, daughters, and other loved ones and the dishonor of their fathers, brothers and tribes or clans. Some family members have come forward to teach the public and especially young people about what terrorists do to their own families. Their stories need constant telling and re-telling.

When the terrorist carries out his mission, the coalition's messages must strip the action of any sense of piety, honor or self-sacrifice. The messages must denude the extremist of all virtues. Instead of honor and glory, the extremist must be shown to thrust grief, disgrace and hardship mercilessly on his family, his people, all Muslims, and the religion itself. Some Muslim leaders will say this publicly, and the job is to amplify the contradiction. The messages must push the reluctant to ostracize or be ostracized.

With Muslim family members worldwide now coming forward not only in grief but denouncing the terrorist attacks, we have even more powerful messages. The young widow of one of the July, 2005 London subway bombers called her husband "naïve," saying that his "mind was twisted" after militants in a local mosque "poisoned his mind." She hinted to a British paper that the extremists tricked her gullible husband. "He was an innocent, naïve, and simple man. I supposed he must have been an ideal candidate," she said, after he began frequenting mosques less than a year before the attacks. "He became a man I didn't recognize." On the morning of July 7, 2005, he kissed his small son goodbye and slipped out without a word to his wife, who was eight months pregnant with their second child.[157]

The message must therefore be targeted to undermine the confidence and commitment of the terrorist's psychological support networks: family members, friends, fellow trainees, fellow terrorists, clans, mosques, schools, scholars, publishers, broadcasters, politicians, clerics and others whose approval, or even non-opposition, are so crucial to the development of the terrorist's state of mind.

As long as there is no credible opposing message – and inefficient action against overt militants – the ideological lock on the terrorist's mind is secure. The U.S. ideological attacks must be rich in imagery and emotion. By attacking the psychological support system on which the would-be terrorist depends, one is undermining the current or future terrorist's own state of mind. Take the ideological

---

[157] Kevin Sullivan, "London Bomber's 'Mind Was Twisted' by Radicals," *Washington Post*, September 24, 2005, p. A19.

war to the neighborhoods to break the network of moral support, both in spirit and in cohesion. Themes, therefore, must fracture the unity of the terrorist's moral support networks by causing doubt and division and breaking the spirit that reinforces the terrorist's own psychological, and often supernatural, determination.

Show that they are on the losing side

The extraordinary quick and unexpected defeats of the Taliban in Afghanistan and of Saddam Hussein's regime in Iraq initially damaged the morale of Islamist extremists who considered the Coalition's immediate victory to be Allah's judgment against them. Decisive armed force thus remains an important option in the hearts-and-minds campaign, but only insofar as it is accompanied by the ideological warfare dimension of the conflict.

Particularly in Iraq, where the U.S. elected not to develop and implement a post-invasion ideological warfare strategy, the decisive war morphed into an indecisive and protracted counterinsurgency that drew out the Iraqi people's agony. Circumstances allowed the terrorists to regroup and soon portray the U.S. and its coalition allies as tramplers of Islam and murderers of Muslim people. Internationally, the U.S. and Britain received more opprobrium than the terrorists.

As of this writing, odds are even that the insurgents and terrorists could win in Iraq, simply by continuing their attrition attacks with roadside bombs on U.S. forces and suicide bombings against Iraqi civilians and relying on political opponents of U.S. leadership, both abroad and at home, to demand unilateral withdrawal. The extremists no longer seemed to be losing. An ideological offensive as described in this section would help show that the extremists are on the wrong side and that the wrong side will be defeated.

Soft side against hard targets: Intra-Islamic persuasion

A surprising softer side to combating extremist ideology is emerging, and its existence should be another part of the message. Islamist politico-religious ideology is so doctrinally weak that clerics who challenge it on theological grounds can actually convert individuals away from terrorism.

In Yemen, home of some of the most extremist teachings, a young cleric and judge named Harmoud al-Hitar and four Islamic scholars challenged al Qaeda prisoners to a debate on theology. "If you can convince us that your ideas are justified by the Qur'an, then we will join you in your struggle," Hitar told the terrorists. "But if we succeed in convincing you of our ideas, then you must agree to renounce violence." As a result of their efforts, between late 2002 and early 2005, more than 360 al Qaeda prisoners reportedly renounced terrorism on theological grounds. "If you study terrorism in the world, you will see that it has an intellectual theory behind it," Hitar said. "And any kind of intellectual idea can be defeated by intellect."[158]

The Yemen case is a rare instance of the use of reasoned logic to disarm the extremist psychologically or individually, and recidivism reportedly was high. However, there was little if any outside support to reinforce and sustain the effort. New messages should overwhelm audiences with the texts, recordings, videos and images of the debates, and by the individual testimonies of each of the 360 former al Qaeda terrorists. The message should stress: "There is a way out."

Amplifying such voices and chronicling the events allows us to highlight the actual war that is occurring within Islam, combating the image that the U.S. and its allies are fighting Islam, and implicitly diminishing the enemy's image of the United States.

Culturally appropriate rhetoric

This point is an appropriate reminder that the messages must be culturally appropriate. That means talking about religion. Frequently, the United States government or its representatives are the wrong messengers, though important agencies and military commands have taken the issue to the extreme of avoiding the issue of religion to the point of obsessiveness. For the purposes of this section, the language of culturally appropriate rhetoric is that of Islam itself, pronounced by faithful Muslims with sufficient moral standing. The United States is not the arbiter of what is or is not Islamic, and U.S. officials must stay away from that question. What officials can do, however, is to highlight the arguments among Muslims for public exposure, and to isolate the extremists. Rather than issue opinions about the inconsistency of terrorist violence with good Muslim principles, the U.S. should merely provide a platform

---

[158] James Brandon, "Qur'anic Duels Ease Terror," *Christian Science Monitor*, February 4, 2005.

and be the amplifier. In so doing, it can regain its credibility as a purveyor of Muslim cultural issues.

The Spanish Muslim fatwa of March, 2005[159] provides an exceptional thematic model for culturally appropriate rhetoric that the United States should amplify and relentlessly repeat in many languages, and encourage those of sufficient standing to emulate. Spanish Muslims enjoy a particular status within Islam by virtue of their descent of what was the Spanish Caliphate of the Middle Ages. The fatwa's strongly-worded messages include:

Terrorism and extremism are un-Islamic.

- ". . . it is necessary to point out that terrorism and extremism contradict human nature and the lessons of Islam."

Muslims who commit terrorism are no longer Muslim.

- "In light of these and other Islamic texts, the terrorist acts of Osama bin Laden and his organization al Qaeda – who look to fill with fear the hearts of defenseless people; who engage in the destruction of buildings or properties thus involving the death of civilians, like women, children and other things – are strictly prohibited and are the object of a full condemnation from Islam."
- "The presence of signs like arrogance, fanaticism, extremism or religious intolerance in an individual or group lets us know that they have broken with Islam and the traditions of the Prophet Muhammad."
- "The perpetration of terrorist acts supposes a rupture of such magnitude with Islamic teaching that it allows to affirm that the individuals or groups who have perpetrated them have stopped being Muslim and have put themselves outside the sphere of Islam."
- "Those who commit terrorist acts violate Qur'anic teachings and thus turn apostates who have left Islam."
- "According to the *Shar'ia*, all who declare *halal* or allowed what God has declared *haram* or prohibited, like the killing of innocent people in terrorist attacks, have become *Kafir Murtadd*

---

[159] Fatwa of the Islamic Commission of Spain, Cordova, March 11, 2005.

Mustahlil, that is to say an apostate, by trying to make a crime such as the murder of innocents, *halal* (*istihlal*); a crime forbidden by the Sacred Qur'an and the Sunna of the Prophet Muhammad, God bless him and serve him."

- "Osama bin Laden and his al Qaeda organization . . . are outside the parameters of Islam; and the same goes for all who wield the Sacred Qur'an and The Prophet's Sunna to commit terrorist acts."

Muslims should not treat terrorists as fellow Muslims.

- "As long as Osama bin Laden and his organization defend the legality of terrorism and try to base it on the Sacred Qur'an and the Sunna, they are committing the crime of istihlal and they have become *ipso facto* apostates (kafir murtadd), who should not be considered Muslim nor be treated as such."

There is no reward in afterlife for murdering non-Muslims.

- "[The Prophet] also said whosoever killed anyone who had signed a treaty or agreement with Muslims, would not smell the fragrance of Paradise. (Sahih Al-Bujari:3166, and Ibn Mayah:2686)."

Muslims who kill other Muslims are unbelievers.

- "These extremist groups bring indiscriminate death, even to other Muslims. We must remember here that The Prophet showed that Muslims who kill other Muslims turn *kafir* (unbelieving)."

In contrast to highly publicized fatwas by their American and British brethren, the Spanish Muslim leaders used very strong language, leaving no room for ambiguity. In doing so, they inflicted the type of harm on terrorist leaders that hurts most: branding them kafir unbelievers. Whereas American rhetorical denunciations and military attempts to kill him enhance bin Laden's image in certain Muslim quarters, fellow Muslims' denunciations of the terrorist as a kafir undermine the terrorist's standing – a tactic which he has criticized and denounced, showing his sensitivity to the word. Labeling the extremists as apostates or nonbelievers makes them fair game to be hunted as terrorists.

The Spanish Muslims also addressed their co-religionists in the next concentric sphere around the terrorist core:

The terrorists' war is unjust.

- ". . . the perpetration of terrorist acts under the pretext 'of defending the oppressed nations of the world or the rights of Muslims' does not have any justification in Islam."

Terrorism is murder,
for which there is no justification.

- "Within the context of defensive warfare, The Prophet imposed strict limits destined to safeguard lives and property. Thus, the Prophet Muhammad prohibited to kill, in the case of warlike conflict, women, children and civilians (Sahih Muslim:1744, and Sahih Al-Bujari:3015)."

True Islamic teaching repudiates terrorism.

- "A correct Islamic formation in madrasas and Islamic universities will allow everybody to understand that Islam is a religion of peace and that it repudiates all acts of terrorism and indiscriminate death."

Extremist teachings twist the meaning of Islam.

- "[Extremist] groups try to conceal their deviation through falsehoods and manipulated interpretations of sacred texts, in an attempt to gain support among Muslims or to recruit new followers. This fraud must be denounced with force by the wise people and leaders of Islam worldwide."

Extremism is damaging to Islam and all Muslims.

- "Muslims must know that terrorism is a threat against Islam and that it is damaging to our religion and to Muslims."

Extremism serves the enemies of Islam.

- "Groups that use names and languages relative to Islam, discredit with their actions the image of Islam and serve the interests of their enemies."
- "Their actions incite islamophobia in countries in which Muslims are a minority, and destroy the relationships of cooperation and neighborliness between Muslims and non-Muslims."
- "Their actions provide a false image of Islam, which is precisely what the enemies of Islam strive to offer the world."
- "Islam is the main victim of terrorist attacks made by some groups that falsely call themselves 'Islamic,' inasmuch as such attacks not only take the life of numerous Muslims, but because they also damage the image of Islam by fomenting feelings of islamophobia and serving the interests of the enemies of Islam."

Having pronounced the extremists as apostates doing the work of enemies of the faith, the Spanish Muslim leaders reached from the innermost to the outer spheres of the ummah, *declaring that all Muslims are duty-bound not to be passive in the war effort, but to fight terrorism and help the authorities.* The importance of these declarations for Muslims in Western countries became clear four months later after the London bombings, when a poll of British Muslims revealed remarkable alienation from civil society, and that one in four indicated that if they learned of a terrorist plot in advance, they would not call the police. Six percent of those polled, equivalent to 100,000 British Muslims, said the London suicide bombings were "fully justified," while the same percentage said that future al Qaeda attacks in Britain would be "justified." According to the fatwa of the Spanish Islamic authorities:

All Muslims have the duty to fight terrorism.

- "The duty of every Muslim is to fight actively against terrorism, in accordance with the Qur'anic mandate that establishes the obligation to prevent corruption from overtaking the Earth."

God holds all Muslims responsible.

- "Do good unto others as God has done unto you; and do not wish to plant the seeds of corruption upon Earth, for God does not love those who sow corruption." (28:77). "The term 'corruption' includes here all forms of anarchy and terrorism that undermine or destroy peace and Muslim security. Muslims, therefore, are not only forbidden from committing crimes against innocent people, but *are responsible before God to stop those people who have the intention to do so*, since these people 'are planting the seeds of corruption on Earth.'" (Emphasis added.)

It is easy to see how the U.S. can fuel the debate and split support from the extremists without injecting the government itself into a theological debate. The only need, in the Spanish fatwa case, was to report on the existence and context of the document, translate and disseminate its contents, amplify the proper voices, and let the debate get going among those with greatest authority and acceptance.

Nothing under United States law prevents government officials, agencies and other entities from:

- *reporting the existence of such declarations;*
- *translating them into all applicable languages as documents of importance in current international political debate;*
- *disseminating them as widely as possible through all public diplomacy and other channels in print, on radio and television, and online;*
- *hosting appropriate commentators to discuss the declarations' relevance in the current international climate;*
- *encouraging or challenging others to address the issues in the declarations from cultural, political or moral perspectives;*
- *challenging people to debate the declarations as vital issues of the day;*
- *reporting on the resultant controversies; and*
- *imaginatively amplifying the messages around the world.*

Conclusion

The concepts, themes and ideas in this volume barely scratch the surface of the messages the U.S. needs to promote. The general conclusion, as the title reveals, is that the United States and its allies must fight the war of ideas like a real war.

That means that the war of ideas cannot be run out of the State Department. State has vital roles to play, and its public diplomacy and public affairs roles are crucial. However, diplomats by their purpose and training are not warriors and should not be expected to become warriors. At the same time, since public diplomacy so dominates the U.S. message-making system and public expectations are so high, the State Department must become far more visionary, innovative, agile and adaptive in delivery of messages to the world. Public diplomacy must be a fundamental part of a counterinsurgency and counterterrorism strategy.

The Department of Defense has taken the lead in transforming the nation's strategic communication with the world. It too has critical roles to play in crafting and delivering America's messages, both of military and non-military natures. The military services have the warfighting mentality that creative and effective message-making requires.

Since this book is about creating messages for the near-term, it is an inappropriate place to discuss bureaucratic processes and structures. The approach in these pages has been to suggest ideas that the U.S. can implement now, with its current bureaucracy, budgets, authorities and decision-making chains.

The most important barrier to break is the false idea that the enemy's ideology is a religion. Radical Islamism is a political ideology whose adherents abuse religion to legitimize their methods and their political cause. Misperception of the foe serves only to undermine the war effort and the overall cause against extremism. It severely limits decisionmakers' freedom of action at the national strategic level. It smothers the initiative of our own diplomats and warfighters to engage the enemy in the appropriate political and cultural battlespaces. It subverts our relations with our natural Muslim friends and allies and their relations with us. To view Islamist extremist ideology as a religious ideology is to believe in the enemy's propaganda and practice unilateral disarmament in the war of ideas. If we continue on that course, the enemy will win.

For now, let innovation and ingenuity take their natural course. Someone, somewhere in the system, civilian or military, should simply lead. If the State Department won't do it, than the warfighters should, as their lives are the ones on the line.

To fight the war of ideas like a real war, the United States must first neutralize and defeat the power of the ideas of the enemy, and subdue the will of others to fight us and our allies. Concurrently but secondarily, the U.S. must work to contain the explosion of anti-American sentiment, and begin to reverse the damage. Only then will world audiences be prepared to accept what should, for the short-term, be a tertiary goal of promoting American values and voices.

Lastly, the private sector has an extremely valuable role to play in this entire effort. Given the realities of how government works, with the inherent slowness, relative inflexibility, and inside-the-box thinking, some of the best solutions have and will continue to originate from private companies, NGOs and individuals. When they do, the U.S. government must amplify those messages and support them in other ways.

The message strategy, then, is a revision of the current public diplomacy strategy, but with emphasis on attacking the enemy:

- Divide, isolate and marginalize the violent extremists by actively, aggressively and relentlessly confronting their ideologies;
- Foster a sense of common interests between Americans and people of different countries, cultures and faiths around the world; and
- Offer people worldwide a positive vision of hope and opportunity that is rooted in America's belief in freedom, justice, opportunity and respect for all.

The Defense Science Board's 2004 report on Strategic Communication provides the larger vision on which the 2005 State

Department public diplomacy strategic direction appears to be based. The Army and Marine Corps' 2006 *Counterinsurgency Field Manual* FM 3-24 provides the warfighters' new doctrine. The three visions can now work together with the right message-making approach: To fight the war of ideas like a real war.

About the author

J. Michael Waller is the Walter and Leonore Annenberg Professor of International Communication at The Institute of World Politics in Washington, D.C., where he directs a graduate studies program in public diplomacy and political warfare.

His practical experience on the ground with U.S.-backed insurgents and counterinsurgents includes serving as an instructor to nearly a hundred commanders of a guerrilla army to help fighters transition, successfully, into a democratic society. He holds a Ph.D. in international security affairs from Boston University and has been a consultant to the Senate Foreign Relations Committee, U.S. Information Agency, U.S. Agency for International Development, and the Office of the Secretary of Defense. He is Vice President for Information Operations at the Center for Security Policy. His articles have appeared in the *Los Angeles Times*, *Readers Digest*, *USA Today*, the *Washington Times* and the *Wall Street Journal*. He is author of *Third Current of Revolution: Inside the North American Front of El Salvador's Guerrilla War* (University Press of America, 1991), and *Secret Empire: The KGB In Russia Today* (Westview, 1994); co-editor of *Dismantling Tyranny: Transitioning Beyond Totalitarian Regimes* (Rowman & Littlefield, 2006) with Ilan Berman; and editor of *Strategic Influence: Public Diplomacy, Counterpropaganda and Political Warfare* (IWP Press, 2007).

About The Institute of World Politics

The Institute of World Politics is an independent, accredited graduate school of statecraft and national security affairs. Based in Washington, D.C., the Institute is dedicated to developing leaders with a sound understanding of international realities and the ethical conduct of statecraft based on knowledge and appreciation of American political philosophy and the Western moral tradition. IWP offers Master's degrees in Statecraft and National Security, Statecraft and World Politics, and Strategic Intelligence. The school's Website is www.iwp.edu.

Made in the USA
San Bernardino, CA
26 March 2018